ETHICAL HACKING FOR BEGINNERS

The practical guide to computer hacking to learn and understand the concept of ethical hacking

Benjamin Crime

ABOUT THE BOOK

Hacker and malicious activity have, in the past few years, been on the rise, specifically in the last one year. The attacks and threats have increased, and the impact on the online world is far-reaching. These attacks have been a source of concern for ordinary internet users and a problem for corporate entities as well. Some of the threats take the form of conventional software, like viruses and malware among scripts, which are aimed at exploiting flaws and achieving various malicious ends.

Hacking has directly impacted the cost of doing business. Many businesses are spending significantly higher amounts of money on online security. Hacker activity targets even the most complex networks as more and more hackers become emboldened in their malicious schemes, and as new skills are developed and perpetrated on internet users. Their primary intentions have always been to compromise business and institutional networks as well as security applications, enabling them to infect computers and unleash viruses and other malicious scripts and programs.

The growing trend in the hacking world is that of mounting denial of service attacks (DoS) against large companies and institutions that primarily rely on the internet for business and even those involved in governance and regulation. Denial of service attacks are achieved by jamming a computer network and making it crash, rendering it incapable of operations or activity. Another method utilized by hackers is mail bombing, which works in a similar manner to denial of service attacks, only targeting mail servers within a network. All these malicious actions are aimed at bringing a business to its knees.

The other form of hacker activity seen has been targeted at secure areas within a network with the sole intention of stealing sensitive data and information. After hacking a network, hackers will move on to steal either by removing or copying sensitive data, which will be used for various purposes. Some will steal credit card information to steal money from individuals, while some malicious groups of hackers will delete data they come into contact with.

Hackers may also create worms, viruses, and Trojans, which are some of the most malicious programs that can be found on the internet. All these programs have the ability to attack computers and networks, corrupt files and sectors in the machine. They can do this by replicating themselves or by attaching to files, ultimately exhausting all available resources.

Preventing hacker activity has thus become one of the most important activities for businesses and computer experts, and ends up utilizing huge amounts of money, potentially in the billions. Even with such investments in IT security and the prevention of hacking activity, it is still an impossible task to curb all hacker activity or stay ahead of the hackers. For personal and home computers, individuals find it easier to curb hacking and related activity through the use of antivirus software.

These different types of antivirus software work very well to scan the computer for infected material, notifying the computer and internet user and neutralizing threats when identified. The need for antivirus software is emphasized especially for people who are constant users of the internet. This becomes very important since most antivirus software comes with a firewall, which forms a strong barrier against hacker activity by keeping the computer safe from outside interference and tampering.

For businesses and the need to protect their networks from hacking, the challenge becomes bigger in terms of resources, expertise, and time involved. In protecting business and company computer networks, much is involved, which begins with a security policy and a host of measures, such as firewalls, intrusion detection systems (IDS), content filtering software, and even more content filtering software among a host of other software aimed at protecting these large networks. It should be remembered that finding protection is an ongoing process, and businesses should continually monitor their networks and invest in software specifically designed to protect the networks.

If you're looking for information on ethical hacking, then read on—I promise to be quick and to the point! Friends tend to raise their eyebrows when I utter the words "ethical hacking" to them. What on earth? Hacking...ethically? And sure, I see their point.

It's bad, right?

Hacking is a "bad" act for sure, or at least when we take the common meaning of the word and in this context. In this case, we really do mean hacking in the sense of penetrating or cracking some kind of computer system in order to gain access to sensitive information. Or to simply cause havoc and crash it. After all, I've heard many folks do this for fun...

However, when we add the "ethical" word into the equation, then the intention behind such "attacks" changes entirely. What we are now talking about is carrying out such attacks for the sole purpose of identifying weaknesses so that we can remove or strengthen them. So it's for the greater good!

Companies may hire individuals or groups to carry out this task. These individuals will be highly skilled in computer systems, networks, social engineering, and so on. Anyway, the point is this: we conveniently refer to this form as ethical hacking. They are doing it with permission, and this is a key part. Don't be thinking you are doing the same thing by "identifying weaknesses" on eBay without them giving your permission first!

Anyway, the good that can come out from this should be very obvious. When companies can discover easy loopholes or entry points in their systems before an actual "nasty" hacker does, they can avoid much embarrassment and financial loss.

TABLE OF CONTENTS

INTRODUCTION

What's a Hacker?

"Hacker" is one of those terms that has a different meaning depending on who uses it. Thanks to Hollywood, most people think a hacker is a person who gains illicit access to a computer and steals stuff or breaks into military networks and launches missiles for fun.

These days, a hacker doesn't have to be a geek from a top university who breaks into banks and government systems. A hacker can be anyone, even the kid next door.

With an ordinary laptop, anyone can download simple software off the Internet to see everything that goes into and out of a computer on the same network. And the people who do this don't always have the best of intentions.

HISTORY OF HACKERS

Nowadays, the word "hacker" has become synonymous with people who sit in dark rooms, anonymously terrorizing the Internet. But it was not always that way. The original hackers were benign creatures. In fact, they were students.

To anyone attending the Massachusetts Institute of Technology during the 1950s and 60s, the term "hack" simply meant an elegant or inspired solution to any given problem. Many of the early MIT hacks tended to be practical jokes. One of the most extravagant saw a replica of a campus police car put on top of the Institute's Great Dome.

Over time, the word became associated with the burgeoning computer programming scene at MIT and beyond. For these early pioneers, a hack was a feat of programming prowess. Such activities were greatly admired as they combined expert knowledge with a creative instinct.

Why Does a Hacker Hack?

Hackers' motivations vary. For some, it's economic. They earn a living through cybercrime. Some have a political or social agenda - their aim is to vandalize high-profile computers to make a statement. This type of hacker is called a cracker, as their main purpose is to crack the security of high-profile systems.

Others do it for the sheer thrill. When asked by the website SafeMode.org why he defaces web servers, a cracker replied, "A high-profile deface gives me an adrenaline shot, and then after a while, I need another shot; that's why I can't stop."

These days, we are faced with a new type of hacker - your next-door neighbor. Every day, thousands of people download simple software tools that allow them to "sniff" Wi-Fi connections. Some do this just to eavesdrop on what others are doing online. Others do this to steal personal data in an attempt to steal an identity.

The Most Common Attacks

1. SideJacking / Sniffing

Sidejacking is a web attack method where a hacker uses packet sniffing to steal a session cookie from a website you just visited. These cookies are generally sent back to browsers unencrypted, even if the original website log-in was protected via HTTPS. Anyone listening can steal these cookies and then use them to access your authenticated web session. This recently made news because a programmer released a Firefox plug-in called Firesheep that makes it easy for an intruder sitting near you on an open network (like a public Wi-Fi hotspot) to sidejack many popular website sessions. For example, a sidejacker using Firesheep could take over your Facebook session, thereby gaining access to all of your sensitive data, and even send viral messages and wall posts to all of your friends.

2. DNS Cache Poisoning

In DNS cache poisoning, data is introduced into a Domain Name System (DNS) name server's cache database that did not originate from authoritative DNS sources. It is an unintended result of a misconfiguration of a DNS cache or of a maliciously crafted attack on the name server. A DNS cache poisoning attack effectively changes entries in the victim's copy of the DNS name server, so when they type in a legitimate site name, they are sent instead to a fraudulent page.

3. Man-In-the-Middle Attacks

A man-in-the-middle attack, also known as a bucket brigade attack or Janus attack, is a form of active eavesdropping in which the attacker makes independent connections with the victims and relays messages between them. This makes the victims believe that they are talking directly to each other over a private connection when, in fact, the entire conversation is being controlled by the attacker. The attacker must be able to intercept all messages going between the two victims and inject new ones. For example, an attacker within reception range of an unencrypted Wi-Fi access point can insert themselves as a man-in-the-middle. Alternatively, an attacker can pose as an online bank or merchant, letting victims sign in over an SSL connection, and then the attacker can log onto the real server using the victim's information and steal credit card numbers.

4. Smishing

Packet sniffers allow eavesdroppers to passively intercept data sent between your laptop or smartphone and other systems, such as web servers on the Internet. This is the easiest and most basic kind of wireless attack. Any email, web search, or file you transfer between computers or open from network locations on an unsecured wireless network can be captured by a nearby hacker using a sniffer. Sniffing tools are readily available for free on the web, and there are at least 184 videos on YouTube to show budding hackers how to use them. The only way to protect yourself against Wi-Fi sniffing in most public Wi-Fi hotspots is to use a VPN to encrypt everything sent over the air.

5. Mass Meshing

Also known as mass SQL injection, this method involves hackers poisoning websites by illegally embedding a redirection JavaScript from legitimate websites previously infected and controlled by the hackers. These JavaScripts redirect the visitor's computer to servers containing additional malicious programs that can attack a user's computer.

The Most Common Targets

Hackers are interested in many types of computers on the Internet. The following list describes different types of targets and their appeal to hackers.

1. Corporate Networks

Corporate computers are often heavily fortified, so hacking into one has high cachet. Behind corporate firewalls are repositories of customer information, product information, and sometimes, in the case of a software publisher, the product itself.

2. Web Servers

Web servers are computers that contain websites. While some contain customer financial information, web servers are usually targets for vandals because they can be defaced to display information the hacker chooses to the public.

3. Personal Computers

With the ever-growing use of Wi-Fi, laptops are becoming one of the most hacked devices. Everything a person visits online can be exposed to someone using software to "sniff" that connection. The website URL, passwords used to log into an online banking account, Facebook pictures, tweets, and an entire instant message conversation can be exposed. It is the easiest form of hacking as it requires little skill.

4. Tablets and Palm Top devices

Tablets, cell phones, and other mobile-ready devices are just as popular as laptops in Wi-Fi hotspots. A hacker in a public hotspot can see a mobile device, as well as all data going into and out of it, just as easily as they can a laptop.

HOW YOU CAN PROTECT YOURSELF

The simple truth is that anyone connecting to the Internet is vulnerable to being hacked. Thus, there is a need to be proactive when it comes to protecting yourself from such attacks.

Sniffing attacks are the most dangerous, as firewalls and antivirus software cannot help. Only a personal VPN can protect a person from a sniffer. The would-be victim, if connected to a personal VPN, has all their data routed through a secure server, making it impossible for the hacker to sniff. A user who has a secure VPN can surf as if he or she is invisible to hackers. PRIVATE WiFi provides such a VPN service.

The methods hackers use to attack your machine or network are fairly simple. A hacker scans for vulnerable systems by using a demon dialer (which will redial a number repeatedly until a connection is made) or a wardialer (an application that uses a modem to dial thousands of random phone numbers to find another modem connected to a computer).

Another approach used to target computers with persistent connections, such as DSL or cable connections, employs a scanner program that sequentially "pings" IP addresses of networked systems to see if the system is up and running. If you have any firewall software, you can see these repeated pings in your log.

Hackers find all these tools, ironically, on the Internet. Sites containing dozens of free, relatively easy-to-use hacking tools available for download are easy to find on the net. While understanding how these tools work is not always easy, many files include homegrown documentation written in hacker shoptalk.

Among the programs available are scanning utilities that reveal the vulnerabilities on a computer or network and sniffing programs that let hackers spy on data passing between machines.

Hackers also use the Net to share lists of vulnerable IP addresses—the unique location of Internet-connected computers with unpatched security holes. Addresses of computers that have already been loaded with a Trojan horse are available for anyone to exploit (in many cases without the owner of the computer knowing).

Once the hacker finds a machine, he uses a hacker tool such as Whisker to identify in less than a second what operating system the machine is using and whether any unpatched holes exist in it. Whisker, one of a handful of legitimate tools used by system administrators to test the security of their systems, also provides a list of exploits the hacker can use to take advantage of these holes.

There are so many conditions that make life easier for hackers. Lax security is one of them—such as when a company uses no passwords on its system or fails to change Windows' default passwords.

In October 2000, hackers broke into Microsoft's system and viewed source code for the latest versions of Windows and Office after discovering a default password that an employee never bothered to change.

Other common mistakes: When system administrators don't update software with security patches, they leave vulnerable ports open to attack. Or when they install expensive intrusion detection systems, some fail to monitor the alarms that warn them when an intruder is breaking in.

Still another boon to hackers is a firewall or router that is misconfigured, allowing hackers to "sniff" pieces of data—passwords, email, or files—that pass through the network.

Once a hacker cracks into a system, his next goal is to get root, or give himself the highest level of access on the machine. The hacker can use little-known commands to get root, or can search the documents in the system's hard drive for a file or email message that contains the system administrator's password.

To protect against these types of attacks, it's essential for individuals and businesses to prioritize cybersecurity. This includes regularly updating software, using strong and unique passwords, monitoring security systems, and properly configuring firewalls and routers. By being proactive and staying informed about the latest threats and best practices, users can significantly reduce their vulnerability to hackers and maintain the security of their systems and data.

Armed with root access, he can create legitimate-looking user accounts and log in whenever he wants without attracting attention. He can also alter or delete system logs to erase any evidence (such as command lines) that he gained access to the system.

In today's environment, millions of people rely on computers to do business, homework, and to dispatch information to others. It is therefore very important to secure the information that we have on our computers. If you are using a computer exclusively, it is your duty to do all you can to reduce computer risks, prevent data loss, and to reduce computer abuse. In the business world, data protection is paramount because a company's data is fast becoming one of the most valuable assets that any company owns. Keeping your electronic data secure from hackers is therefore most important.

A computer security risk is any action, deliberate or otherwise, that could cause loss of information, damage to critical software, or data corruption. Computer security risks also extend to program incompatibilities or computer hardware obsolescence. Many instances of computer loss or computer damage are planned and are therefore not accidental. Any intentional breach in computer security is said to be a computer crime, which is slightly different from a cybercrime. A cybercrime is really an illegal act perpetrated through the Internet, whereas a computer crime involves any illegal behavior that involves the use of a computer.

There are several distinct groups of people involved in computer crimes, and understanding who they are is important. The most popular form of criminal computer acts is broadly known as hacking. In this case, a person uses a network or the Internet to gain illegal access to a computer. Hackers, too, have gained much notoriety over the last 10 years because they are seen as representing people who are in rebellion against the systems of society. Some of the more recent names assigned to people posing computer security risks are cracker, cyber-terrorist, cyber-extortionist, unethical employee, script kiddie, and corporate spies.

The term hacker was actually used in reference to ordinary people with the ability to break into computer systems legally. However, with the widespread use of the Internet, a hacker has now become known for illegal actions. A hacker is defined as someone who accesses a computer or computer network unlawfully. They often claim that they do this to find leaks in the security of a network. Recent developments in computer programming have spawned the term Ethical Hacking. This is an IT-related term for posing as a thief to catch loopholes in your own computer systems. The term cracker has never been associated with something positive; this refers to someone who intentionally accesses a computer or computer network for unlawful or unethical purposes.

A cyber-terrorist is someone who uses a computer network or the internet to destroy computers, websites, or systems for political reasons. The intention here is to cause harm to important systems such as a banking system or a military computer network in order to score political points. Unlike a regular terrorist attack, cyber-terrorism requires highly skilled individuals, thousands of dollars to implement, and many months of planning. The term cyber extortionist is used to refer to someone who uses emails or other electronic communication media as an offensive weapon. As an example of this, a cyber-terrorist can access a web-based database, confiscate it, and erase other available copies. They can then demand a ransom for the release of this information.

They could carry out their illegal act by doing other things such as sending a company a very threatening email. The information they may have could be trade secrets, company data, or even personal information about one of the senior officers of the company. By demanding a ransom for not releasing such information through the internet, they are participating in cyber-terrorism against the company or persons.

Many computer security risks are directly related to disgruntled employees. It is for this reason why many of the top companies in the USA have adopted sections of the Sarbanes-Oxley Act of 2002. Executives of each public company must take personal responsibility for the security of a company's data in addition to truthfulness in accounting practices. All stakeholders must be assured that the data which a company has about a person, such as credit cards, must be secure at all times. As the internet grows, only time will tell what other measures will become necessary to reduce computer risk, thwart cyber-terrorism, and mitigate the impact of hackers and crackers all over the globe.

After you have been on the internet for some time, you will realize a few terms often used have to be really understood fully. Such terms are web strategy, webmaster, and web broker. At first glance, some may not think it is of relevance to them. But these are the areas we should know if we have a site that we call our own. Then we come to the question: how much can we control what we think we own?

The virtual or online presence is not very real, and it involves many links in between for each business to reach others. Recently, I have received many emails in almost all my inboxes from sites that claim I subscribed to them.

These unnecessary emails led me to find out what some online terms mean. I have listed the meanings of some below and realized that it is easy to scam anyone into thinking I am running a business when, in reality, I am unemployed. The web is a place where we have to be careful of our beliefs, just like in the real world. The only consolation is that the online presence is at arm's length and not in person.

The internet can scam people just so some hackers or mischief-makers can get easy money. The extent of morality in us shows the extent of the lack of greed. An online site went as far as saying they would not know if a subscriber subscribed twice to the same site. This means that they do not know who pays them for what. In such a scene, I have closed the sites I own. If mentioning names amounts to slander, then what are the unethical strategies called? For example, the email I received today, the 13th of January 2010, says someone is the beneficiary of thousands of dollars but does not mention any name. This really is the height of joblessness. Technology is used for spam. The email is posted on my WordPress blog named bhuvan108.

This email has no name on it but is sent to me with a subject termed "update from Lexus Corporation." Technology has its pitfalls, as seen in my blog. I prefer to learn before I earn and have made an attempt to understand some terms listed below.

Web Brokers
Web brokers offer interactive marketing and web management consulting services to site owners searching to develop and strengthen their online business.
A transaction must be made between two members. Such an exchange can be done through a broker.
There are discrete dealings, advisory dealings, and executive dealings for these jobs.

Web Master

A webmaster, also called web developer, site author, or website administrator, is a person responsible for maintaining a website. The duties of the webmaster may include ensuring that the web servers, hardware, and software are operating accurately, designing the website, generating and revising web pages, replying to user comments, and examining traffic through the site.

Webmasters may be generalists with HTML expertise who manage most or all aspects of web operations. Depending on the nature of the websites they manage, webmasters typically know scripting languages such as PHP, Perl, and JavaScript. They may also be required to know how to configure web servers, such as Apache, and serve as the server administrator.

Web Strategy

A web strategy is a long-term strategic business plan indicating how to create and develop a company's online presence adhering to the business development strategy. Depending on the business maturity, immediate needs, and long-term goals, the programmer should yield different results.

THE PRACTICAL GUIDE TO COMPUTER HACKING

Computer hacking is a process of accessing a computer intentionally without any kind of authorization. It modifies the programs on the system in order to accomplish a goal other than the original purpose of the computer. Cracking passwords, extracting important information stored, and decoding files are all part of the computer hacking process. Professionals who master this art are popularly known as hackers.

As the two sides of a coin, hacking also has its own pros and cons. In the present day competitive world, many companies hire hackers as an important part of their technical group to ensure the security of their company's key essentials. In the business war, there are many who try to extract important information and data of renowned companies through hacking. Therefore, it becomes really significant for companies to hire hackers. Such hackers are true technical buffs and take this job with a desire to master this art and get into the depth of computer technology. Some renowned hackers like Dennis Ritchie, Ken Thompson, and Shawn Fanning made significant contributions to constructive technological advancements.

The innovations created by them, like the UNIX operating system by Dennis-Ken and Napster by Shawn, were breakthroughs in the computer industry. This positive side is truly beneficial to one and all.

On the other hand, computer hacking can be negative in many ways. There are hackers who play fraud and intrigues for various disparaging purposes like breaking security code to access unauthorized networks, stealing personal information, altering financial data of a company, stealing significant business information, breaking computer security, extracting bank details of an individual, and enjoying unauthorized access to systems. Hacking can be more destructive if any kind of national security information or confidential government data is exposed. Apart from this, there are many destructive activities a hacker can perform for his or her own benefit. This side of hacking is very gloomy and can lead to many computer-related crimes.

There are many ways that can be used to prevent the negative activities of hacking. The first and most important way is to install antivirus software that helps in blocking the way of hackers from uploading malicious files onto the system. Avoid using simple passwords for any important data stored on the system or for accessing online bank accounts. It is always recommended to use a combination of alphabets and numbers that is usually difficult for hackers to figure out. A password involving the name of an individual, the name of the company, or any birth date can easily be decoded by hackers. Delete all kinds of suspicious emails received from an unknown sender and also avoid using P2P file-sharing software.

If used for a constructive purpose, computer hacking can be a blessing, but when it comes to destructive activities, it is a curse. Everyone using a computer at home or office should be smart enough to make a wise judgment to ensure high levels of computer security.

FACTS ABOUT ETHICAL HACKING

Ethical Hackers are also called the "good guys" or "white hats." In the ancient days where the good cowboys wore the "white hat" for identification, they were popularly known as the good guys. An Ethical Hacker is a person employed by a company to hack into their network before an illegal hacker attempts it. The purpose of doing this is to know if their network security is strong and solid to prevent an illegal Hacker from attacking their network. Many people don't want to hear the word hacking because they believe that hackers are bad guys. But ethical hacking is much different. The good guys hack into a system or network, but before doing this, they must have gotten permission from the company whose system is being attacked.

Ethical hackers play a crucial role in ensuring the security of a company's digital infrastructure. By identifying vulnerabilities and potential attack vectors, they help companies take proactive steps to strengthen their security measures. This process, known as penetration testing or "pen testing," can reveal weaknesses that could be exploited by malicious hackers.

Organizations of all sizes, across various industries, can benefit from ethical hacking. By employing these skilled professionals, they are able to stay one step ahead of cybercriminals and protect their valuable data and systems. As technology continues to advance and cyber threats become more sophisticated, the demand for ethical hackers will likely increase, making it a critical component of comprehensive cybersecurity strategies.

The company and the ethical hackers enter into a strong legal contract that will last for many years. The agreement of the contract is what transforms an illegal act into a legal act. The company doesn't like losing hackers because they are the backbone of the company, and it will affect the company negatively. Companies pay a lot of money to secure hackers because they know that they have privileged access to highly sensitive information of the company, which they might use against them if they are not treated in a good manner.

Companies should thoroughly assess the background of any ethical hackers they are employing. This hacker will have privileged access to highly sensitive information. The company must have 100% total honesty and trust in their good guys.

When people first hear about hacking, they will usually see this idea as something negative. Indeed, hacking has always been about taking advantage of unprotected or weakly-guarded sites or systems for the individual's own selfish interest. Because of this, others (often companies) who want to strengthen the protection of their online systems turn to professionals for help. These professional hackers (sometimes known as "white hats") use an ethical hacking methodology to help build a stronger defense against real hacking threats. By deliberately "attacking" the system, they can quickly identify its flaws and then begin to come up with contingency plans to stall, avoid, or eliminate real actual hacking attacks.

From the ethical hacking methodology, you can see that not all hacks are bad. The act of hacking ethically into a system in order to expose possible weak points, ones that real hackers, or "black hats" (due to less savory intentions) can exploit, can help prevent the company from loss of earnings or reputation. Indeed, a lot of companies are now seeking the services of those who can perform this task because they understand that the only way to fight against skilled hackers is with another skilled hacker of their own!

Those with a strong understanding of computer systems can train to carry out these services. Though when you consider the ethical hacking methodology includes breaking into online systems, it is quite possible that many white hats today have gained their experiences originally as black hats themselves! So long as your actions have been permitted by the company who owns the system, the mischief or disorder that you'll create during the hacking process will entirely benefit the company so long as they follow up and eliminate those weaknesses.

Ethical hackers are either hired professionals who have made a name for themselves as black hat hackers or are real employees of the company who are knowledgeable enough to perform the task. This is not about good or bad hackers, white hats or black hats; ultimately, it is about the benefit of the company and the protection of sensitive data they may hold. If you had a less desirable past (black hat) but have since decided to work for the system than against it, you will be well cared for because of the service you can now provide.

The ethical hacking methodology is all about getting results when it comes to protecting online systems against destructive attacks. You are concerned only with keeping the assets and interests safe, and only by thinking and acting like a true hacker can this be achieved.

Without a doubt, this is an effective way to protect from online threats. If you're a company, do not hesitate to hire a white hat hacker, because they are equipped with the right knowledge and skills to combat a threat from another hacker. On the other hand, if you're involved in hacking yourself, perhaps there would be a career for you to consider in working on the other side?

This process is done by computer and network experts called ethical or white hat hackers. These people analyze and attack the security system of an organization with the intention of finding and exposing weaknesses that crackers can exploit and take advantage of. It is important to understand that unlike crackers, ethical hackers get permission from the relevant authority to go on and test the security of their information system. Crackers cause harm and loss to an organization and negatively affect the integrity, availability, and confidentiality of an information system. So how did the concept of ethical hacking come up, and how is it done?

The field of ethical hacking has been in the computer world for a while now. Today, this subject has continued to gain much attention due to the increasingly availability and usage of computer resources and the internet. This growth and expansion of computer infrastructure have provided another avenue for interaction and, so, has attracted major organizations in businesses and governments. These bodies want to fully take advantage of the benefits offered by technology so that they can improve the quality of service they offer to their customers. For example, organizations want to use the internet for electronic commerce and advertising among others.

On the other hand, governments want to use these resources to distribute information to its citizens. Even though they want to utilize this new potential that has been enhanced by technology, there is a fear of security. Organizations fear the possibility of their computer information system being cracked and accessed by unauthorized people. On the other hand, potential customers and users of these services worry about the safety of the information they are prompted to give. They fear that this information, like credit card numbers, social security numbers, home addresses, and contacts, will be accessed by intruders or outsiders who are going to use their data for other purposes outside the one that was intended. By so doing, their privacy is going to be interfered with, something that is not desirable to many people if not all.

Due to the above raised fear, organizations sought to find a way to approach and counter this problem. They came to discover that one of the best methods they can use to limit and control the threat posed by unauthorized personnel to a security system is to employ independent professionals in security matters to try the security measures of a system. In this scheme, hackers use the same tools and techniques used by intruders, but they do not damage the system nor do they steal from it. They evaluate the system and report back to the owners the vulnerabilities their system is prone to. They also recommend what needs to be done to the system so as to make it more secure.

As evidenced from above, ethical hacking go hand in hand with security strengthening. Though it has done much in increasing security matters, still more needs to be done. It is impossible to obtain absolute security, but even though, doing nothing to computer security is dangerous and undesirable.

We know that our modern technology is not as foolproof and reliable as we hope it will be when we really need it. We've watched it fail, causing train crashes, plane crashes, and even luxury cruise ships to run aground. We've watched our space rockets meet their demise, and we've even been advised that our electric cars, laptops, and other equipment might burst into flames at any time. We trust all of our technology, but only to a point. Yes, and maybe that is wise - take GPS for instance - yes, let's talk, shall we?

There was a troubling article in the International Business Times titled "GPS Terrorism: Hackers Could Exploit Location Technology To Hijack Ships, Airplanes," by Ryan W Neil published on July 29, 2013. In this article, we find a computer scientist grad student quite impressed with himself for hacking a luxury yacht. He took over its GPS navigation system and could therefore command the yacht to go wherever he wished it. That is pretty good for bragging rights considering there is a hacking convention coming up, but it also points to the dark side, the black-hatter-hackers, and even terrorism.

If hackers can hijack the GPS system of wayward vessels, especially those of large size and shape such as cruise ships, container ships, large tankers, or various cargo ships, they can cause a world of hurt. Not to mention a small ecological environmental disaster. A ship sunk at the entrance to a port or maritime choke point could cause intense logistical problems. Think about the Panama Canal, the Suez Canal, or even the Houston channel. What if someone hacked into a luxury yacht and tried to ram a military ship?

No, the damage done would not be as dire as you might think because the military ship is very strong. Would the captain of the military ship order to open fire if it was going to get rammed by a private vessel? He'd or she would have every right to, but would they dare? What if there were friends and family of notoriety on that vessel?

If all the luxury yachts everywhere have similar GPS systems, and many of them do, then they are all in jeopardy now. Often these special GPS systems are on cargo ships so they can pass each other in the night without hitting one another or navigate very closely at maritime choke points without the risk of collision.

Indeed, this would be a terrorist's dream, wouldn't it? Wouldn't it be better if this grad student hadn't alerted the media, or told all his friends for bragging rights? Wouldn't it have been better if he didn't do it at all, or if he did it only in conjunction with a GPS company he was working with to help them better their system? Some people use very bad judgment, unfortunately, all of us may have to pay for it one day. The computer scientist should have gone about this differently. What transpired is unacceptable. Please consider all this and think on it.

The Global Positioning System (GPS) unit is taking a high toll in the latest addition of gadgets and electronic devices. GPS is a satellite-based electronic device that provides information on time, positioning, and weather conditions. Sometimes the satellite navigation system may not be pre-installed, but you can connect it separately to your device. GPS devices can be loaded in cars, mobiles, home computers, laptops, digital cameras, or smartphones.

How does the GPS device work?

Each device has an inbuilt GPS receiver connected to the GPS satellite that coordinates the location and shows the position. The security forces and security system of countries have become largely dependent on GPS navigation systems. The military defense, civil, navy, and aviation forces are using GPS systems to track, coordinate, and regulate the locational activities. The excessive use of GPS to track positions has made it more vulnerable to hacking. Attack on Global Positioning System for hacking and hijacking is on the rise. Installed GPS devices have enabled easy hacking of smartphones, iPhones, laptops, and cars, and last but not the least is aircraft hijacking. Through GPS, jamming a hacker can get complete remote access to the electronic device.

How Can a GPS Device Be Jammed?

The purpose of GPS jamming is to block the signaling and prevent it from working. To disable a GPS tracking device, a variety of methods are used. Hackers using mobile phones and other radio signal-related electronic devices can disable the GPS too, and not only that, they can replace the real GPS signal with a fake one. This will show a fake locational position. These GPS spoofing gadgets actually send fake radio signals replacing the real signal transmitted. Many people tend to relate GPS signals with navigation. The use of GPS as a time signal has potentially made it more susceptible to GPS spoofing, which posed as a bigger threat today rather than simple GPS blocking.

How do you protect your GPS device?

That is a big question. Ethical Hacking Institutes are building technically sound experts who can actually prevent you from hackers. These ethical hacking training centers run certified ethical hacking courses. You can hire certified ethical hacking individuals who can technically and exclusively devise programs for you to protect your GPS system. Interloping, manipulating or nullifying of a GPS device is a punishable offense. So be on your guard and stay well informed and aware if you are technically and professionally dependent on the Global Positioning System. Remember, whatever GPS device you have, it is always prone to hacking.

In today's digital world, small, medium, and big businesses are facing the biggest threats from hackers. Any computer hacking attack, if successful, can create a lot of problems for networks and in fact, all the critical information stored in the various computers within the network. In the field of IT, there is a growing need for professionals having ethical hacking courses to work for them and provide security to their computers and networks. Known as white hat hackers or ethical hackers, these professionals are experts in the area of anti-hacking techniques. They work for preventing the motives of malicious hackers from stealing or damaging important data and ensure the safety and protection of computer systems and networks.

People with ethical hacking training work to provide security to IT systems. At times, if required, ethical hackers can even break into any other system. But the reason for doing so must be a genuine one for the safety of an organization or company. In fact, both black hat hackers and white hat hackers do the same thing, but the major line of discrimination is that an ethical hacker has altruistic motivations.

There are many major threats and issues related to computer hacking that one must be aware of to understand Information Security in the true sense of the terms. Today, there are some basic threats that you may face as an individual or as an organization such as:

- Theft of passwords
- Email-based threats
- Email-based extortion
- Launch of malicious programs (Trojans)
- Internet time theft

Here are some major corporate threats that need to be handled by professionals having knowledge of ethical hacking and lots more:

- Web defacement
- Corporate espionage
- Website-based launch of malicious code cheating and frauds
- Exchange of criminal ideas and tools
- Cyber harassment
- Forged websites

Not only this, there are also some online threats that need to be taken care of, such as:

- Email spamming
- Theft of software, electronic records, computer hardware, etc.

- Cyber stalking
- Email bombing
- Morphing
- Denial of service attacks

Apart from this, there are some other threats too related to computer hacking, such as:

- Theft of information
- Email forgery
- Theft of e-cash, credit card numbers, online banking accounts, etc.

Protecting your computer and network can be done by ethical hackers, but as far as security is concerned, the first step is to secure the hardware on which all the valuable information is stored and by which it moves across the network. Basically, it means limiting who is able to actually touch the computer and what a person can do with it if they do gain on-site access. To protect your computers, network, and data from all types of damage and loss that can be done through computer hacking, however, physical security can make a lot of difference. Well, in physical security, computers must also be properly protected from natural disasters and accidental damage in addition to deliberate acts.

THINGS HACKERS DO WITH THE INFORMATION THEY STEAL

A question that we hear a lot when it comes to cybercrime: What are hackers after, anyway? There are a lot of different types of hackers and computer scammers out there, so there's no one answer. Some of them are just practical jokers, some use viruses to get revenge on the company they were fired from or just to bother random people online. The main reason hacking exists, however, is that it's a great way to make a dishonest living by stealing information from unsuspecting users.

If you have the know-how, the time, and the lack of moral scruples, it's really not that hard to crack into someone's computer with a spybot and monitor their activity, or even to take control of their computer from afar and look right into their files.

So now the question becomes "Why?" Why do hackers want that information so badly? There are a number of things a hacker can do with the information they steal from you. The most obvious example would be, of course, that they can steal your financial information or your identity, using your credit card number to buy whatever they like or even getting into your bank account.

That's the scariest kind of hacker, anyway, but even if you don't have any of your financial information on your PC, you're still a target for info and identity theft.

Besides outright stealing your identity and spending your

hard-earned money for you, many hackers will settle for some more mundane details, such as using spyware to look at your browser history, email, internet proxy, anything they can get ahold of, and then selling that to unscrupulous advertisers who flood your inbox with spam and fill your screen with pop-ups.

Back when computers were more of a hobby than a serious part of one's everyday life, we really didn't have much info on our PCs worth stealing. In those days, viruses were relatively benign. Maybe they'd make your computer do something weird, maybe pop up an image or a message, like THE CREEPER, the first computer virus, which simply made your computer monitor read "I'M THE CREEPER, CATCH ME IF YOU CAN". For the most part, they were harmless practical jokes.

There still are those practical joker hackers out there, but what hacking has largely become is an illegal multimillion-dollar-a-year industry, a great way for con artists to make a quick buck without even having to put themselves at risk by lying to your face.

The bottom line is that hackers want money, and they don't care how they get it. If they can take your bank account information, they will, and if they can't, they'll settle for some personal info to sell to spammers.

Luckily, a good security program will generally protect you from most hackers, but they're working around the clock to figure out how to bypass your security measures, how to find new weak points, so it's important that the methods you use to protect yourself evolve at a faster pace than that of the hacker's methods.

PROTECTING YOUR WEBSITE FROM HACKERS

Hacking attacks are a constant worry and perennial headache for any network administrator. More interestingly and ironically, the best defense against them comes from hackers themselves. But these hackers are of a different kind and breed - they are 'ethical hackers'.

While companies and government organizations all across the world are spending huge sums on hiring professional network security experts or ethical computer hackers, you can make your computer secure by being a little more careful and by keeping your system equipped with next-generation anti-hacking solutions.

Let's see how:

1. Always use the latest version of anti-virus software applications. With good anti-virus software, whenever a hacker tries to access your machine, you would be warned about it so that you can take necessary steps before any damage is done.

2. Always keep the firewalls in active mode as it will prevent unauthorized entry by the hackers.

3. Keep checking the programs running on your system on a regular basis. In case you come across some program that you might not have installed or which does not form part of standard operating system, then be alert and cross-check it as it might be some sort of spam.

4. To minimize risk against virus attacks and hackers, keep your operating system up to date as it allows the machine to be aware of the latest discovered security holes. If you don't do that, you are just giving an open invitation to the hackers who just evolve from every failed or 'taken care of' hacking attack.

5. Never ignore the patches when they arrive for installation. Usually, what happens is that a hacker makes a way to enter your computer through some common programs. By installing security fixes and patches, you make your computer safe from hackers as they are developed with the sole motive to fix security-related issues.

Well, these tips are just the primary precautions to keep your system safe from the hands of hackers. But it's better to take the help of experts to take care of security measures. Many companies nowadays employ ethical hackers with knowledge of network security, cracking, and hacking to counter the menace of criminal hacking.

Let me explain a little more. Hackers are broadly categorized into three groups:

- Black-hat hacker: These are the malicious or criminal hackers that break into networks or computers, or create computer viruses.

- Grey-hat hacker: These are skilled hackers who have mixed characteristics of white and black-hat hackers. They usually hack for fun or challenge but in the process can do some pretty damaging things.

- White-hat hacker: These are ethical hackers whose task is to provide security and protection to IT systems. Such people are employed by companies to enhance their IT security and keep their network systems free of hackers and spammers.

Ethical hacking is thus fast becoming a chosen career option for young IT pros given the fact that the IT security market worldwide is growing by leaps and bounds. There are various courses available for computer hacking and network security training. Professional cracking tutorials and other courses prepare IT security pros for attractive careers in big organizations.

If you are a website owner, it is one of your top priorities to make your website secure from malicious attacks and hacking. In fact, when setting up your website, whether you are making an online store, a business website, a blog, or a website you use to make money online, you should not just think about design, traffic, and content, but also about how to protect your website and make it trustworthy to online visitors.

To learn how to protect your website, here are a few tips and ideas on making sure your site would not be hacked and attacked.

- Make it a habit to have long passwords and make sure they are alphanumeric. A 10 to 12 character password is strongly recommended. Also, avoid those that are obvious to guess like birthdays and anniversaries. If you are worried about a higher chance of forgetting them, write it down and keep it in a secure place or hide it somewhere that only you can access it. You can also change your password often for your safety and protection.

- Configure your firewall. Your firewall helps screen the incoming information that comes into your system by blocking unauthorized access, depending also on how you configure it. To be properly protected, make sure that your firewall is properly set according to your security needs. Take note that if not properly configured, your computer's firewall can be the hacker's door towards your system.

- Make sure your anti-virus software is updated. Your first line of defense is an anti-virus software that can help you ward off malicious attacks and viruses, especially those that will allow hackers to control your computer.

- Have your site tested by ethical hackers. Aside from installing anti-virus software as your first defense on how to protect your website, you can also seek the services of ethical hackers to help you do some penetration tests on your website. This way, you will know the vulnerability of your site, and you can find solutions to that early on.

- Make sure you have checked and validated all inputs to your site. Cross-site scripting is one weakness of websites that can be used by hackers by inserting scripts into your webpage that may lead to their access to confidential information and the likes. To protect your site and information and ward off hackers using this technique, you have to check and validate inputs to your website. If you allow online visitors to input some data on your website, you have to validate each entry and check it against what inputs are allowed. Look for extra scripts and be wary of the type and length of the inputs.

Indeed, there are people who hack websites just for the fun of it. Most of them may be doing it for money or hate. You may never know their reasons but you can do something to prevent them. Indeed, learning how to protect your website is a priority that will save you a lot of money in dealing with a hacked website.

As a website owner, is there anything more terrifying than the thought of seeing all of your work altered or entirely wiped out by a nefarious hacker? We see data breaches and hacks in the news all the time. And you may think, why would someone come after my small business website? But hacks don't just happen to the big guys. One report found that small businesses were the victims of 43% of all data breaches.

You've worked hard on your website (and your brand) – so it's important to take the time to protect it with these basic hacker protection tips.

HOW TO SECURE YOUR WEBSITE FROM HACKERS

You may have been worried when starting this post that it would be full of technical jargon that your average website owner would find baffling. Some of our tips further down do get technical, and you may want to bring in your developer for those. But there are a few things you can do on your own first that don't involve that much technical know-how.

Step #1: Install security plugins. If you built your website with a content management system (CMS), you can enhance your website security with plugins that actively prevent website hacking attempts. Each of the main CMS options have security plugins available, many of them for free. Security plugins for WordPress:

iThemes Security
Bulletproof Security
Sucuri
Wordfence
fail2Ban
Security options for Magento:
Amasty
Watchlog Pro
MageFence
Security extensions for Joomla:
JHackGuard
jomDefender
RSFirewall
Antivirus Website Protection

These options address the security vulnerabilities that are inherent in each platform, foiling additional types of hacking attempts that could threaten your website. In addition, all websites – whether you're running a CMS-managed site or HTML pages – can benefit from considering SiteLock. SiteLock goes above and beyond simply closing site security loopholes by providing daily monitoring for everything from malware detection to vulnerability identification to active virus scanning and more. If your business relies on its website, SiteLock is definitely an investment worth considering.

Note: Our Managed WordPress hosting plan has SiteLock built in, along with other features to help secure your site.

Step #2: Use HTTPS. As a consumer, you may already know to always look for the green lock image and https in your browser bar any time you provide sensitive information to a website. Those five little letters are an important shorthand for hacker security: they signal that it's safe to provide financial information on that particular webpage.

Example of green lock for certificate

An SSL certificate is important because it secures the transfer of information – such as credit cards, personal data, and contact information – between your website and the server. While an SSL certificate has always been essential for ecommerce websites, having one has recently become important for all websites. In July 2018, Google Chrome released a security update that alerts website visitors if your website doesn't have an SSL certificate installed. That makes visitors more likely to bounce, even if your website doesn't collect sensitive information.

Search engines are taking website security more seriously than ever because they want users to have a positive and safe experience browsing the web. Taking the commitment to security further, a search engine may rank your website lower in search results if you don't have an SSL certificate.

What does that mean for you? If you want people to trust your brand, you need to invest in an SSL certificate. The cost of an SSL certificate is minimal, but the extra level of encryption it offers to your customers goes a long way to making your website more secure and trustworthy.

At HostGator, we also take website security seriously, but most importantly, we want to make it easy for you to be secure. All HostGator web hosting packages come with a free SSL certificate. The SSL certificate will be automatically applied to your account, but you do need to take a few steps to install the free SSL certificate on your website.

Step #3: Keep your website platform and software up-to-date

Using a CMS with various useful plugins and extensions offers a lot of benefits, but it also brings risks. The leading cause of website infections is vulnerabilities in a content management system's extensible components. Many of these tools are created as open-source software programs, making their code easily accessible to both well-intentioned developers and malicious hackers. Hackers can scrutinize this code, searching for security vulnerabilities that allow them to take control of your website by exploiting any platform or script weaknesses.

To protect your website from being hacked, always ensure your content management system, plugins, apps, and any installed scripts are up-to-date. If you're running a website built on WordPress, you can quickly check whether you're up-to-date when logging into your WordPress dashboard. Look for the update icon in the top left corner next to your site name. Click the number to access your WordPress Updates.

Step #4: Make sure your passwords are secure

This one seems simple, but it's crucial. It's tempting to choose a password you know will always be easy for you to remember. That's why the #1 most common password is still 123456. You must do better than that — much better than that to prevent login attempts from hackers and other outsiders. Make an effort to create a truly secure password (or use HostGator's password generator). Make it long. Use a mix of special characters, numbers, and letters. And avoid potentially easy-to-guess keywords like your birthday or child's name. If a hacker somehow gains access to other information about you, they'll know to guess those first.

Holding yourself to a high standard for password security is step one. You also need to ensure everyone who has access to your website has similarly strong passwords. One weak password within your team can make your website susceptible to a data breach, so set expectations with everyone who has access. Institute requirements for all website users in terms of length and types of characters. If your employees want to use easy passwords for their less secure accounts, that's their business. But when it comes to your website, it's your business (literally), and you can hold them to a higher standard.

Step #5: Invest in automatic backups.

Even if you do everything else on this list, you still face some risk. The worst-case scenario of a website hack is to lose everything because you forgot to back up your website. The best way to protect yourself is to ensure you always have a recent backup. While a data breach will be stressful no matter what, having a current backup makes recovery much easier. You can make a habit of manually backing up your website daily or weekly, but if there's even the slightest chance you'll forget, invest in automatic backups. It's an affordable way to buy peace of mind.

Steps to Secure Your Website from Hackers

All of the above steps are relatively painless, even for website owners with minimal technical experience. The second half of the list gets a little more complicated, and you may want to call a developer or IT consultant to help you out.

Step #6: Take precautions when accepting file uploads through your site. When anyone has the option to upload something to your website, they could abuse the privilege by uploading a malicious file, overwriting one of the existing files important to your website, or uploading a file so large it brings your whole website down. If possible, simply don't accept any file uploads through your website. Many small business websites can get by without offering the option of file uploads at all. If that describes you, you can skip everything else in this step. However, eliminating file uploads isn't an option for all websites. Some types of businesses, like accountants or healthcare providers, need to give customers a way to securely provide documents. If you need to allow file uploads, take a few steps to ensure you protect yourself:

- Create a whitelist of allowed file extensions. By specifying which types of files you'll accept, you keep suspicious file types out.
- Use file type verification. Hackers try to sneakily get around whitelist filters by renaming documents with a different extension than the document type actually is, or adding dots or spaces to the filename.
- Set a maximum file size. Avoid distributed denial of service (DDoS) attacks by rejecting any files over a certain size.
- Scan files for malware. Use antivirus software to check all files before opening.
- Automatically rename files upon upload. Hackers won't be able to re-access their file if it has a different name when they go looking for it.
- Keep the upload folder outside of the webroot. This keeps hackers from being able to access your website through the file they upload. These steps can remove most of the vulnerabilities inherent in allowing file uploads to your website.

Step #7: Use parameterized queries. SQL injections are among the most common website attacks that many sites fall victim to. SQL injections can occur if you have a web form or URL parameter that allows external users to provide information. If you leave the parameters of the field too open, someone could insert code into them, gaining access to your database. It's crucial to protect your site from this because of the significant amount of sensitive customer information that may be stored in your database. There are several steps you can take to safeguard your website from SQL injection attacks; one of the most important and easiest to implement is the use of parameterized queries. Utilizing parameterized queries ensures your code has specific enough parameters so that there's no room for a hacker to tamper with them.

Step #8: Use CSP

Cross-site scripting (XSS) attacks are another prevalent threat that site owners need to be vigilant against. Hackers may find a way to inject malicious JavaScript code onto your pages, which can then infect the devices of any website visitors exposed to the code.

Part of the effort to protect your site from XSS attacks is similar to using parameterized queries for SQL injections. Ensure that any code you use on your website for functions or fields that allow input is as explicit as possible in what's allowed, so you're not leaving room for anything to slip in.

Content Security Policy (CSP) is another useful tool that can help protect your site from XSS. CSP enables you to specify which domains a browser should consider valid sources of executable scripts when on your page. The browser will then know not to pay attention to any malicious script or malware that might infect your site visitor's computer.

Implementing CSP involves adding the appropriate HTTP header to your webpage that provides a string of directives telling the browser which domains are acceptable and any exceptions to the rule. You can find details on creating CSP headers for your website here.

Step #9: Lock down your directory and file permissions

All websites can be boiled down to a series of files and folders stored on your web hosting account. Besides containing all the scripts and data needed to make your website work, each of these files and folders is assigned a set of permissions that control who can read, write, and execute any given file or folder, relative to the user they are or the group to which they belong.

On the Linux operating system, permissions are viewable as a three-digit code where each digit is an integer between 0-7. The first digit represents permissions for the owner of the file, the second for anyone assigned to the group that owns the file, and the third for everyone else. The assignments work as follows:

4 equals Read
2 equals Write
1 equals Execute
0 equals no permissions for that user

As an example, consider the permission code "644." In this case, a "6" (or "4+2") in the first position gives the file's owner the ability to read and write the file. The "4" in the second and third positions means that both group users and internet users at large can only read the file – protecting the file from unexpected manipulations.

So, a file with "777" (or 4+2+1 / 4+2+1 / 4+2+1) permissions is readable, writable, and executable by the user, the group, and everyone else in the world.

As you might expect, a file assigned a permission code that gives anyone on the web the ability to write and execute it is much less secure than one that has been locked down to reserve all rights for the owner alone. Of course, there are valid reasons to open up access to other groups of users (anonymous FTP upload, for example), but these instances must be carefully considered to avoid creating a website security risk.

Step #10: Keep your error messages simple (but still helpful).
Detailed error messages can be helpful internally to help you identify what's going wrong, so you know how to fix it. However, when those error messages are displayed to outside visitors, they can reveal sensitive information that tells a potential hacker exactly where your website's vulnerabilities are.

Be very careful about what information you provide in an error message, so you're not providing information that helps a bad actor hack you. Keep your error messages simple enough that they don't inadvertently reveal too much. But avoid ambiguity as well, so your visitors can still learn enough information from the error message to know what to do next.

Securing your site and learning how to protect against hackers is a big part of keeping your site healthy and safe in the long run! Don't procrastinate taking these important steps.

Why Companies Need Ethical Hacking and Better Cyber Security

While talking about hacking, what do we tend to imagine? A silhouetted figure in a hoodie typing something on a computer, a black screen, innumerable codes, a dark room, right? In movies, it takes just a few seconds to breach a system and obtain all the data. But in reality, it takes lots of effort and persistence to carry out the procedure called 'hacking.'

It takes immense hard work, skills, knowledge, and passion to become a professional ethical hacker. Now, the question arises: how can interfering with someone else's database be ethical? Although it sounds like an oxymoron, it is true that the world needs white hat hackers now more than ever before. Business entities, law enforcement agencies, and government bodies are in need of skilled professional ethical hackers.

With the advancement of technology, such as IT outsourcing, cloud computing, and virtualization, we are exposed to various security threats every day. In that case, networking experts are hired to protect the database of a particular organization from potential harmful exploiters. Data exploitation can lead to significant damage to reputation and financial loss for any company. Now, ethical hacking is one of the most popular security practices performed on a regular basis.

Cybercrimes have increased massively in the last few years. Ransomware like WannaCry and Petya make headlines every day with their various variants, and it would not be an exaggeration to say that they are here to stay, increasing their muscle power to cause more harm. Phishing schemes, malware, cyber espionage, IP spoofing, etc., are now prevalent. In order to safeguard data, companies need to adopt a proactive stance.

With the ever-increasing popularity of cloud technology comes the baggage of security threats. Now, when business organizations use cloud services like Google Drive, Microsoft

Azure, or Dropbox, they are actually storing sensitive data on a third-party tool, which may or may not work in their best interest. Using third-party file-sharing services allows the data to be taken outside of the company's IT environment. This often leads to several security threats, including losing control over sensitive data, snooping, key management, data leakage, etc.

Almost all of us are active on various social networking sites. We actively share our whereabouts, interests, addresses, phone numbers, and dates of birth there, and with this information, it is easy for cybercriminals to figure out the victim's identity or steal their passwords. A study reveals that around 60,000 Facebook profiles are compromised every day. Social media users are likely to click on anonymous links shared by friends or someone they trust. This is an old method of exploiting the victim's computer

The definition of network forensics and ethical hackers has evolved over time. Many organizations have yet to realize that the cost of protecting their company databases is much less than dealing with a severe cyber-attack to recover all data. Prevention is always better than cure. Network forensics and ethical hackers are hired in IT sectors to continuously monitor and identify potential vulnerabilities and take action accordingly.

Organizations must incorporate advanced layered defense and multiple threat detection engines to detect and mitigate threats at the earliest stage. Do not fall into the trap of fancy threat tactics. It is time to take serious action to defeat cybercriminals at their own game.

Judging by the title, many company owners and heads of

technology departments are scratching their heads and wondering why they would want to be hacked. There are a great many people who have never heard of ethical hacking and who only think that hacking is a terrible thing and something to avoid. The fact is that this type of interference in a computer system can actually save a company millions!

One of the most important reasons for ethical hacking is for security purposes. How can a company know just how safe their in-house network is against truly damaging hacking? A company can hire cybersecurity experts who will hack into the network and find the insecure areas, so that the company can take the necessary steps to make sure they become more secure. Checking for security leaks covers two distinct areas. These are threats from actual hacking into employee or customer files and leaks that allow in viruses that can shut down an entire network in just minutes. Both of these leaks can cost a company a great deal of money, so this is a very important service. Typically, the individuals performing these tasks are knowledgeable in cybersecurity and trained as ethical hackers.

A company that is hacked or attacked by cybercriminals is going to lose business, as their customers are going to lose faith in them. If the customers do not feel that their information or personal details are completely safe, they are not going to purchase products or services anymore. This can break a company in just a few weeks of the information being taken. Viruses can be even more damaging. While personal information that is stored may not be shared out this way, the stored information can be lost along with other important documents such as invoices, payroll, and company records that are archived. It only takes one virus to wipe out an entire hard drive full of data.

The other reason for conducting this type of approved computer breach is to train the IT personnel to spot these weaknesses on their own and to keep them up to date on the latest security software. When there are employees who can spot these holes in the security, then they can be caught much quicker. The problem can be alleviated before it becomes an issue and no records are going to be lost or stolen. The technology in computer systems and networks is constantly advancing. Older systems must be patched. Companies need to stay up to date by hiring penetration testing companies to conduct ethical hacking to ensure that the network is safe and protected. Having personnel who can also do this is a wise choice for any company that relies on a computer network for day-to-day business.

SOLUTION FOR THOSE WHO HAVE BEEN A VICTIM

We get this question several times a week, so it's not just you. And no, it doesn't mean you're crazy - even if your friends think so, and even if law enforcement won't take your case. People's computers and phones get hacked every day.

Why won't the police do anything about it - isn't it a crime?

In general, law enforcement will take on a case that involves endangerment of children, loss of more than about $500 in property (this changes from jurisdiction to jurisdiction and can include intellectual property), a believable threat to Homeland Security, or a clear threat to the safety of your person - like a death threat, for instance.

They may take on cyber-stalking if it is part of a violation of parole or a court order. Otherwise, they'll be needing you to furnish more evidence, such as that provided by a private investigator or computer forensic expert, before they'll take on a case. The police are just too busy with a limited budget.

Before you decide what you need to do about it though, you need to decide what you want to do about it: Do you just want it to stop, or do you want to catch the person who's doing it? Or both?

It's not really possible to be online and be 100% protected from hacking, but there are numerous measures you can take to make it not worth most anyone's time.

They include:

- Keep your operating system and antivirus patches updated.

- Secure your router - especially your wireless router: The manufacturer or your Internet Service Provider can help you with the best settings for your particular equipment.

- Don't give out your Social Security number or use it as an ID: You usually only have to give it to your employer, your financial institution, and government agencies.

- Disable your Guest account on your computer.

- Don't make your personal info public on social networks or elsewhere.

- Don't open email from people you don't know.

- Don't click on links in email.

- Don't make online purchases from sites you don't know well.

- Use a firewall (hardware and/or software).

- Make sure that your Android is not rooted and that your iPhone is not jailbroken.

- Don't give any of your passwords to others.

- Don't use the same password for everything.

- Make sure that Administrator access on your computer is protected and accessible only to you (use a password).

- Disable Guest access on your computer.

- Disable remote logins.

- Require a password to log onto your computer, phone, or email.

- Use effective passwords: A good guide is at the "Perfect Passwords" page at Gibson Research Corporation's website.

- If you've already been compromised, you can sometimes roll back your system via System Restore to a time before the compromise - if you know when that was. You may just want to back up your important documents, format your hard disk, reinstall your operating system, and get a clean start.

- On an iPhone or a BlackBerry, a factory restore will wipe out any old virus, keylogger, or other malware you might have picked up - along with everything else that you put there on purpose. Doing the same for an Android should wipe out any malware as well. Although some Android data may be recoverable by an expert after a factory reset, there should be no active malware.

But, have I been hacked?
Frankly, it's not always easy to tell.

Most apparent phone, email, or computer hacking is really the result of nontechnical "human hacking." We make so much information public, it can become possible for a perpetrator to guess logins and passwords or fool an email service into sending a password reset link for an account that is not theirs. One well-publicized recent example is Matt Honan of Wired Magazine, who famously wrote, "In the space of one hour, my entire digital life was destroyed." But nobody used any special technical skills. They just looked up information, made some clever guesses, and had a lot of chutzpah. Fortunately, most of us are not such attractive targets as a Wired journalist.

What are some signs that could indicate you have been hacked?

1. New programs have been installed on your computer - ones you didn't install (although some software - especially free software - sneaks various programs and "helpful" browser

toolbars past you).

2. New documents appear on your computer.

3. Documents disappear from your computer (although it's not hard to accidentally delete or move files around without noticing).

4. Programs pop open that you didn't click on (although there are other, innocent reasons this could happen).

5. You get odd pop-up messages that don't seem to come from a program you are using.

6. Your passwords have changed (and not because you just forgot them).

7. Your security program(s) has been uninstalled or deactivated.

8. The computer is doing things by itself - the mouse moves and clicks on things without any action by you, for instance.

9. You find information about you on the web that should only be known to you.

10. There's a note displayed on your desktop - your screen - that you didn't put there.

What should I do if I see some of these?

Document everything you see, with dates and times, and take screen shots right away. For screen shots, it's easiest to use your cell phone camera if it's handy, but it can be done right on the computer.

In Windows, press the PrtScrn key (to put an image of the whole screen into your clipboard), then open a new document (such as in Paint) and press Ctrl-V (to paste the image into the document), then save it with a meaningful name, like "Screenshot at 1:27PM on Jan 1, 2023."

On a Mac, simultaneously press the Command (cloverleaf) key, the Shift key, and the number 3. The screen is saved to your desktop with a date and time as the name.

You can report an incident to the Internet Crime Complaint Center at ic3 dot gov, and if it is what the government would consider a dramatic incident, some action may be taken.

What do forensics people do for clues to try to catch the perpetrator, or generate enough evidence so that the police will take it and run with it?

1. Freeze the evidence in time with a forensic image.
2. Search the device for keyloggers, rootkits, Trojans, remote control access, bash history.
3. Search out meaningful IP addresses.
4. Search out meaningful email addresses.
5. Check Administrative and Guest User accounts for vulnerabilities.
6. Find deleted files that may be relevant.
7. Inspect Volume Shadow Copies and System Restore Points for relevant evidence.
8. Search the entire device (used and deleted/unallocated space) for text that may have been noticed or may be relevant.
9. Help to identify found IP addresses.

Step 1: Scan local machine for Malware:
This is an obvious prevention measure, but often overlooked by most people. A majority of customers we speak to that have been victims of a hack previously had no security products installed on their machines, and those that did often had them

installed out of the box, barely configured, forgotten about, and seldom updated.

If you don't have a decent virus/malware product installed on your desktop, make an informed purchase by discussing your specific needs with various vendors. Ensure that it's set to automatically scan your machine each day. Ensure that at least each week it connects to the vendor's site and updates itself with new libraries of virus and malware definitions.

If you want to get bonus points, install software that allows you to monitor your network traffic and investigate when you see odd outgoing requests. Your machine should never be contacting the outside world without you either expressly taking an action or setting up something like a regular download of new virus definitions. If your machine is randomly connecting to addresses or sites you know nothing about, then "Houston, we have a problem!"

Step 2: Rotate FTP passwords:

File Transfer Protocol (FTP) provides full access to your files on the server. Like all passwords, you should not set these and forget about them. They should be updated regularly. We recommend monthly if you access your FTP regularly, but if you access it less frequently, it should be okay. If you've never changed passwords, we suggest that you update it now! You should also have a reasonable password policy.

This involves:

• DO NOT use the same passwords for everything
• DO NOT use dictionary words, or people's names

• DO NOT re-use the same passwords. Once used and rolled, discard!

• DO use a random password generator

• DO use a minimum of 8 characters

• DO use a combination of uppercase, lowercase, numbers, and symbols.

Step 3: Rotate database passwords:

Your database password is what allows your website to access your database. It's not as critical as rolling the admin password for your application or FTP details, but it's still an important part of a well-managed password policy. We recommend bi-monthly password changes for this, though you may want to adjust the frequency depending on specific circumstances.

The most likely scenario if database access is compromised is that a bad actor could create a new admin user for your site, delete your database completely, or modify content that is stored and served from the database. If you do change this password via a management interface like the Webgyan Console or cPanel, you need to remember that your website has to have the new password configured into it. Generally, you'll have an interface for this, or some applications require you to edit a text-based configuration file on the server. It sounds complicated, but once you know your way around, it's a 5-minute task.

Step 4: Remove access details:

If you took your car to the mechanic and left the spare keys so they can work on it, you wouldn't leave them the keys after you pick it up. Why would you leave full access to your site once work or changes are completed?

You should hand access details out strictly on a required-use basis. Once the work is done, go through Steps 2, 3, and 14. If you have given domain-level console access, also go through Step 5.

Some of you don't outsource your development work and have dedicated IT staff. Any time a staff member with a specific level of access leaves, you should reset those details immediately. Remember, you are doing this not because they may deliberately do something nasty, in fact, that's generally unlikely, but as a precaution in case at some point in the future their computer was exploited or compromised.

We backup data so that in the case of a disaster we are able to get all customers back online.

Step 5: Rotate 'TheConsole' (or cPanel) passwords:

This is a very easy step. Simply follow the instructions to reset your control panel passwords. Use the same common sense as described in Step 2 to set a more difficult password.

Step 6: Subscribe to external monitoring:

This is like an insurance policy. Companies like Secure do a range of really neat things for you. They'll scan your site each day, and immediately alert you if you've been compromised. They offer services where they will clean your site if you do get compromised and you need immediate help. If you are using WordPress, they'll do preventative monitoring for you, so you are alerted to updates in the application, plugins, themes, and the like.

Step 7: Backup of web files:

There is a notion that your hosting provider will have backups ready and waiting for you to access and can immediately recover all your lost data, without any charge. Generally speaking, hosting providers don't do backups for the reason you think. We backup data so that in the case of a disaster, we are able to get all customers back online. The backup sizes we deal with are in the many terabytes. So I recommend in the strongest possible terms to BACKUP!

It's a simple task that will save you from a lot of headaches later. There are even applications available that are able to backup. Backing up doesn't have to happen every day, but with a busy site, weekly backups should be part of your strategy. For websites that are static and change very rarely, monthly backups are more appropriate. No matter what schedule you decide to follow, if bad things happen, you will at least have a copy of your site and you can easily republish quickly, without hassle and at no charge. So what are you waiting for? If you've never backed up, do it now, and then come back!

Step 8: Backup of database:

This is simply an extension of Step 7. If you have a site that signs up new users, for example, an e-commerce website that requires shoppers to register before purchase; you most likely market to them, run a loyalty program or have some kind of reward scheme. What would happen if all that data was deleted? If you have a busy site, you may decide weekly is too infrequent and decide to archive a copy of your database daily.

Again, there are many tools available that will do this for you automatically, especially if you are using very common database technology like MySQL. Restoring from a self-generated backup is a 5-minute job. Getting your hosting provider to trawl through archives and do a restoration for you will leave you off the air for multiple hours in a best-case scenario.

Step 9: Review software for patches:

You should proactively keep your website up to date as best

as possible. This one would seem self-explanatory, but it's probably the most common way for a site to get exploited and is largely ignored. It's safe to say that most people tend to forget to update their website, with the usual process of having your website built by a developer, who then hands it over to you, and that would be the last time the site is updated. Ever.

We routinely see CMS or e-commerce sites that have not been updated for 3+ years, and often 5 years. So by the time a piece of software is 3 years old, it's generally ancient. If it's then compromised, fixing it becomes 10x more complicated, as there isn't a straightforward upgrade path from the version you are on to the latest. It is therefore not just a simple patch install; instead, it involves trying to re-engineer the whole thing while your site is offline, and you are losing money. This becomes a very bad thing. Most software companies have mailing lists that you can subscribe to, and they notify you each time security vulnerabilities are discovered, new patches, and new versions and the like are available.

Step 10: Review installed add-ons:

An extension of Step 10. Again, a very common scenario we see is a site owner or manager who thinks they are doing everything right by updating the core site software. But they forget all about the add-on modules that have been installed. It's a bit like leaving the house, locking the doors, but leaving the windows wide open.

Step 11: Review any installed templates or themes:

Same as Step 11. Again, very often overlooked and another common way to exploit your site.

Step 12: Rotate site admin passwords:

It's always important to change the admin password for your site regularly. Some hackers will create themselves a new admin account and use that to do harm to your website. Check regularly for any accounts that you haven't created, especially those with admin privileges.

Step 13: Review logs & scan for high traffic:

A common method for hackers to gain access to the admin section on your site is to write a program that tries to log in using a list of commonly used admin passwords. Many people don't ever change the default install password, 'password', or 'default', or cunningly change it to something like 'password123'. You can see where this is going.

Let's say your admin site is at the address, test.com. In your raw server logs, if you see large numbers of visitors to that page, especially from single IP addresses, then it is safe to assume that people have or are trying to do bad things.

The method used in Step 13 can assist here. As can putting your admin section of the site, if possible, into a directory that isn't called 'admin'. These little things can be very helpful.

Step 14: Review all file permissions:

Unix file permissions can confuse even very technical people, so we won't try to explain them in the context of this guide. If you are interested, the reference provided will give you a basic primer. In a nutshell, file permissions dictate who is allowed to do what with individual files. The 'what' part is defined as being able to read the contents of a file, to write to the contents of a file, or to execute a file - computer lingo for making the file do something.

Very often, when trying to build an application, it's easier to relax file permissions instead of fixing your code. While this makes it easier to get the code to run, it also opens up significant security holes. If you have files and directories that are set to '777', which means read by anyone, write by anyone, and executed by anyone, this is mostly a very bad thing. Your files and folders should have file permissions in place that are just enough for the website to do what it needs. If they exceed those permissions, depending on the application, you or your developer should look at carefully restricting them.

If you got this far, well done! I hope this post has helped you. If it has or you feel there was more information that could be added, we're always happy to take feedback.

Being hacked can be a daunting and overwhelming experience, not to mention sometimes detrimental to your business if your website is down for long periods of time. However, precautions can be taken to mitigate the consequences, with the most important ones being to back up your files regularly, rotate your passwords, and ensure regular updates to all software on your site and server. You should then be able to have a backup of your site up and running in no time, while trying to figure out how and why the hack occurred.

ETHICAL RISK MITIGATION

Those who have worked hardest and longest at risk mitigation say that they experience this work as analytically and intellectually demanding in ways they could not have predicted going in.

Meanwhile, others see no need for anything new, claiming that risk-control work, where it really is necessary, should simply be delegated through existing line-management structures, with each functional manager or process owner being required to identify and handle the risks within his or her own areas.

This approach breaks down at the earliest possible stage— when executives ask for risks or problem areas to be nominated for attention. When the risk-control function is simply delegated down the line, managers will generally identify only those risks of which they are aware, which align neatly with their functional or program areas, and which they are happy to disclose.

By adopting more formal risk-management structures, agencies are better able to deal with the risks that are invisible or uncertain, unrepresented or under-represented in their normal process flows, awkward in shape and size (thus not falling clearly within the responsibility of anyone official or department), or shared (where cooperation with other agencies is a prerequisite for effective intervention).

International and global risks are larger-scale or higher-level risks than the available control mechanisms. Global warming, emerging infectious diseases, genocide, and international terrorism are good examples.

Effective action is limited by the absence of any central control mechanism or any legal mandate or authority to act on a sufficiently broad front. Inevitably, where conscious opponents are involved, the "control" business turns into a continuous, dynamic game, played against opponents intent on outwitting the control operation. Examples of such opponents include terrorists, drug smugglers, fraud artists, hackers, and thieves.

There may also be "conscious" opponents such as viruses that mutate and evolve through invisible risks. These are those which, by conscious design or by some quirk of their nature, do not reveal themselves. Their magnitude is usually uncertain, resulting in serious under-investment in control.

Examples of harms that often go unreported or under-reported include: corruption; extortion; drug dealing; date rape; fraud; gambling; prostitution; many forms of white-collar crime; and crimes within the family. Reliance on international treaties and voluntary cooperation between agencies, organizations, and nations makes it difficult to divide the work, the costs, and the credit among the contributing parties.

Control operations exist in an environment of multiple and competing perspectives on the problem, often without any effective political process to resolve them.

Control strategies must always take opponent adaptations into account. Winning the control game requires close monitoring and study of the opponents' moves, along with understanding and undermining their strategies. Risk control becomes a game of intelligence and counter-intelligence, such as addressing sexual or physical abuse.

To tackle such risks, an agency must first uncover them. Systematic measurement is a critical first step in developing an effective control operation. Proactive and intelligence work are vital for scoping and detection—for helping to reveal the true nature and extent of the risk and ensuring that interventions are designed around the whole of the risk rather than the tip of the iceberg.

Risks where prevention is paramount involve unthinkable disasters—for instance, nuclear or biological terrorism.

It is extremely difficult to estimate the probabilities and magnitude of the risk. This makes it hard to set the budget for control. The norm is serious under-budgeting. It is inherently problematic to justify the cost of such work, given the absence of visible disasters. It is also difficult to measure preventive performance.

When performance is enhanced by risk-taking, the culture may reward and even celebrate excessive risk-taking by those who can achieve results and "get away with it." Pressure for performance may impel employees to "drive close to the edge," to the brink of disaster.

For far too long, managing risk has been seen as an esoteric business function—designed to control losses and adhere to compliance standards. But as more organizations fall prey to complex intangible risks, from unwanted disclosure due to rampant cyber threats to breaches of conduct driven by skewed incentive systems, the aperture of risk management is expanding from protecting the balance sheet to promoting ethical leadership and values-based decision-making.

Consider Yahoo, with its record-breaking cyber breach estimated at more than 500 million records, or Wells Fargo, facing unwanted public excoriation after creating thousands of fake customer accounts, or the Volkswagen emissions scandal or the warning signs that could have prevented the Germanwings disaster. Many of these failures were either fueled by or lost in the byzantine maze that is the modern enterprise, which often breeds a combustible mix of indifference and short-termism. Complex systems fail in complex ways, but all start with human failings.

Senior business leaders and their boards must therefore change the way they think about risk and how they respond to it. Rather than countering complex risk with an even more complex risk management system, which comes with its own blind spots and brittle places, leaders have to equip the individuals in their charge with common levels of risk awareness, codes of conduct, and value systems.

To do this, I've often relied on a handful of maxims. While it's true that maxims can sometimes sound cliché – like a phrase on a motivational poster that employees walk past every day but never really look at — they can also be useful if leaders put real effort into them. Here are a few that I have found most useful in fostering a healthy sense of risk-awareness in organizations in which senior managers are also demonstrating ethical leadership:

Values matter most when they are least convenient. In an environment riddled with uncertainty and variability, value systems are meant to be the only constants. However, all too often they are proven to be meaningless words in an annual report. For value statements to be more than empty slogans, they must withstand the trial by fire of tough calls guiding behavior and decision-making when it is least convenient. The now-famous Tylenol recall of the 1980s is an enduring example of how Johnson & Johnson's credo guided decision-making in a time of crisis. A small number of firms are counter-intuitively becoming activists about championing their value systems, even at the risk of short-term shareholder returns. No one gets extra credit for doing the right thing when it is easy.

Bad things happen in the dark. Ethical lapses arise when people take risks but do not bear the downside of their risky behavior. These hazards are most prevalent where they can be most easily hidden – such as in remote locations, less-supervised business units, or on understaffed teams. Misaligned incentives can also create organizational "blind spots." Wells Fargo's massive account-fraud scandal illustrates the insidious effects of incomplete employee incentives that turn a blind eye to unethical behavior.

Combating issues like these begins with transparency and accountability. When information is shared quickly and openly across the organization, bad dealings can be rooted out before they spread. It's a leader's responsibility to shine a light into any dark organizational corners.

Privacy is a luxury. In the age of pervasive cyber-risk and unwanted disclosure, consistently aligned behavior is the best defense. All it takes is one employee clicking on one sketchy link in one email for an organization or institution to be infiltrated by anyone from a disgruntled employee, to WikiLeaks, to nation-state actors. The recent large-scale denial of service attack that affected internet stalwarts like Amazon, Twitter, and PayPal by exploiting connected devices underscores that the amount of money spent on cyber security is not a proxy for greater defense. The Clinton campaign spent months of time and effort atoning for statements made in emails sent through Hillary Clinton's private server and continues to respond to emails hacked by, allegedly, the Russian government and leaked through WikiLeaks. Apparently, the hackers were able to get access to the emails when campaign chairman John Podesta clicked on a phishing link.

Today, risk lies between the chair and the keyboard. Given that breaches are now seemingly inevitable, risk managers might need to spend less effort trying to prevent the next hack and more time reminding employees not to include embarrassing or sensitive information in easily-breached communications in the first place.

Remoteness breeds indifference. Attitudes toward risk are deeply informed by the tone, tenor, and remoteness of the top. Leaders who practice what they preach, have conviction, and lead by example are better at managing risks than those who merely pay lip service to ethics, value systems, or codes of conduct. Simplicity is key in addressing this gap. When senior leaders encourage bounded risk-taking and show that they are open to hearing bad news, they can help hone an organization's muscle memory on how to respond to emerging threats. When those executives, conversely, dismiss details as too "in the weeds" for their attention, show that they don't want to hear questions or bad news, or are simply impossible to ever track down in the hallways, moral lapses become more likely.

GUIDES TO PROTECT YOUR BLOG FROM HACKERS

It's nothing like going into your WordPress blog and finding that it has been hacked. One of the worst attacks is the Pharma Hack, as far as I am concerned, because it is so vicious. It targets your best-indexed posts and places anchor text that leads back to sites that sell Viagra and Cialis. These hackers are creating juice and backlinks off the blog owner's hard work, and there are thousands of victims on the web; some may not even know that they have been victimized.

Once you have been attacked, your first course of action may be to do a search in WHOIS to find out who is the owner of the sites in the anchor text. You may find the information, but in many cases, the site owner's name, address, and telephone number may be fake. When you call the hosting company, they will not be able to help you. They usually will tell you that there is nothing they can do and suggest that you take legal action.

So what should you do? How can you keep this from happening to you?

A strong password would be a start, and from time to time, you should change your password. When creating your blogs, don't use the default username as "admin"; come up with another username.

One thing that you should do as a WordPress blog owner is to make sure you keep your blog updated. Ensure you upgrade to the current version of WordPress, and your plugins should also be updated.

You should also periodically backup your files and your database as well.

Can you protect your computer from all possible viruses and other invasions?

The quickest answer to this is "no." It's just flat impossible to protect your computer from all viruses, registry attacks, worms, spyware, malware, popups, and other such nasties.

That's the bad news.

The good news is that you can clean up and protect your computer against almost all of these undesirable intruders.

The first thing you need to do is download a program called Mozilla Firefox. It's a newer and better browser than anything offered by those guys in Seattle. For one thing, hackers have been concentrating their efforts on Microsoft products like Internet Explorer and MSN Explorer. This makes these browsers more likely to be attacked, whereas Firefox, at least as of this writing, seems more secure. And it does offer great popup protection.

Another thing you will like about Firefox is a feature called Tabs that lets you have numerous web pages up at the same time with the ability to click back and forth between them. For example, you could have your favorite site, eBay's homepage, a phone number directory, the Merriam-Webster Dictionary, and your favorite blog all loaded at the same time... then just click amongst them as the moment moves you.

Here's what you'll really like about Firefox. It's free from Mozilla.org, which is a sort of consortium of public-minded software engineers who develop and distribute freeware (free software). Mozilla is also responsible for a great, free email program called Thunderbird.

Thunderbird is a fast and efficient way to get and send email and has great spam filters. I've personally been using it for more than a month and haven't gotten a single piece of spam mail to date. Compare this with the stuff you get when you use other free email services such as MSN Hotmail.

Before you install either of these programs, you will want to rid your computer of any nasty software it has fallen victim to. A good way to do this is to download another great, free program, Ad-Aware SE from Lavasoft (Lavasoft.com). This program detects and eliminates objects such as a registry invasion. The Webopedia defines your registry file as "a database used by the Windows operating system (Windows 95 and NT) to store configuration information." A registry invasion happens when a "free" program changes your registry to automatically load spyware or some undesirable program. For example, a website called iMesh allows you to download free programs, share files, and search for music and videos... but will alter your registry file to incorporate a service called GAIN (GAIN Publishing) that you may find very annoying.

Ad-Aware will also find and eliminate known data-mining programs, aggressive advertising, parasites, and scumware, as well as selected traditional trojans, dialers, malware, browser hijackers, and tracking components.

You can also find and eliminate spyware with a program called Spybot Search & Destroy. It's available for free at spybot.info/en/index.html. Install this program and then click on Search & Destroy, and it will scan your hard drive in a matter of moments and then show you a list of "problems" it has found. It also tells you the type of problem, for example, "registry change."

Once the scan completes, all you have to do is click on a button titled "Fix selected problems." Spybot will first create a restore point (in case you delete something you wish you hadn't) and then fix all the problems that are checkmarked (if there is any problem you do not want fixed for some reason, just remove the checkmark next to it).

There is a great anti-virus program you can also get for free. It is AVG Free Anti-virus and is available at Grisoft.com. AVG will scan your hard disk, then report and eliminate any viruses found. In addition, it automatically downloads information on new viruses from time to time to help keep you protected. This automatic download service is free as well.

For a blogger, threats from a hacker are a very real possibility. Every day there are so many blogs around the World Wide Web, which are hacked by hackers. This causes havoc in the life of the blogger since he loses all his work and a source of revenue from the blog. A blog is especially vulnerable to hackers if it has a good Google Page Rank, Alexa Rank, etc. In other words, a popular blog is more at risk of getting hacked.

After all the effort you put into your blog, you are earning quite a sum of money for yourself every day. You SEO-ed your domain, bought your own domain name, optimized your domain for Google AdSense, and everything, and you are a happy person. One day after you come back from work/ school/whatever, you log in to your blog, and suddenly your blog is not what it used to be anymore.

Is your blog being hacked?

Today, I will be talking about steps you should take to protect your blog from potential hacker attacks. This guide contains the basics of how you can protect your blog. I hope that these steps will be simple enough for everyone to understand; if not, you can always ask me.

1. Get an anti-virus program and update its database regularly

Sometimes there are 'bugs' or 'defects' in your anti-virus programs, and if you do not update them regularly, hackers may take advantage of the situation and compromise your blog's safety.

2. Use your anti-virus program to scan your computer regularly

Even with the anti-virus program installed, it is still possible that there are still traces of spyware/malware/adware left in your computer. Destroy those things, and hackers will have a harder time cracking your blog.

3. Install a Firewall on your computer

Install a Firewall program on your computer to prevent unwanted transfer of files across the hackers' computer and yours.

4. Be careful of the websites you visit, especially adult ones

Adult websites are riddled with malicious viruses. Do not

go there if you can because it is possible that these viruses can come onto your computer without you knowing.

5. Destroy spyware with your anti-spyware program or prevent it with the said Firewall

Spywares are viruses that hackers use to get your sensitive information and use it for their own benefit. Destroy them with your anti-spyware programs before they destroy you.

6. Be self-conscious when disclosing your personal information to anyone on the web

Make sure that the websites you buy your products from or use their services are trustworthy websites. Internet scams are rampant, so make sure you only give your personal information to the companies you can trust.

7. Follow the news on computer virus outbreaks

Like an old saying goes: it's always better to prevent yourself from the problem than to cure it when you get one.

Anti-virus

Always have a trusted and regularly updated antivirus installed on your system. There are many great antiviruses available, such as McAfee, Symantec, etc., to name a few. Make sure that all the updates of the antivirus are installed so that it can be on top of the latest threats that are lurking on the internet. Many Trojans and malware can gain access to your system and thereby your personal information if you have weak protection from your antivirus. Having an effective and updated antivirus is the most basic step to ward off hackers.

Password

Many bloggers wish they had made their password stronger and more complicated. Unfortunately, for many, it becomes too late because their blog usually has already been hacked. Completely avoid using your name, celebrities, or any particular word. Hackers aim at the victim's password most of the time to hack into their blogs. So, as a preventive measure, always make use of long, abstract, and alphanumeric passwords for your login credentials. This will help you enhance your online security a long way. And of course, other basic precautions include never sharing your password with anybody except, of course, those on your team or whom you trust personally.

Ethical Hacking

If you think that you have hack-proofed your blog, then maybe you would want to test it. Especially if your blog is authoritative, there is a high possibility for hackers to target your blog; in that case, you should test your blog for vulnerability against hackers. You can do this by hiring ethical hackers who would be carrying out test attacks for you; they can then offer suggestions for further improvement for your security against hackers.

The World Of The Ethical Hacker

A Pen Test, or Penetration Test, is carried out by what is referred to as a White Hat or Ethical Hacker. But who and what exactly defines an Ethical Hacker? For the most part, a White

Hat or Ethical Hacker is a computer expert who possesses the programming knowledge to recognize vulnerabilities within an operating system and network. What separates them from the world of the Black Hat Hacker is their intent. An Ethical Hacker intends to secure a system by recognizing vulnerabilities and providing the solution to reduce, if not remove, that vulnerability. A Black Hat Hacker, on the other hand, has every intention of exploiting vulnerabilities for their own mischievous ends. Even so, White or Black, they are all effectively hackers!

The Good Guys

More and more organizations are turning to professional IT Security experts to carry out Pen Testing on their systems and networks, ensuring risks are lowered and data remains as secure as possible. An Ethical Hacker is the 'good guy'; however, the methodology they use and knowledge they possess is used to circumvent security and, in some cases, actually crash those systems, as is the case with Black Box Testing. Nevertheless, it is ethical because the ultimate goal is to increase the security of those systems. In addition, an Ethical Hacker is doing this by request.

The Logic Of It All

The logic is that if an Ethical Hacker can penetrate the system during a Penetration Test, so can a Black Hat hacker. It takes one to know one, which may leave you wondering how and why an IT Security expert might enter the world of Penetration Testing. The answer is varied: there are those who turned a new leaf (so to speak), and there are those who have always worn the White Hat and are quite simply extremely good at their job. They have the computer savvy to analyze systems and code, possess insight with regards to the 'mind' of the Hacker, and also have the knowledge it takes to solve issues. In a way, not dissimilar to those detectives who possess the ability to 'understand' the criminal mind but not the inclination to be one. It simply doesn't follow that all Hackers have a 'criminal mind'.

Ongoing

Pen Testing invariably calls for a talented IT Security professional who is creative and can think outside the box. While more and more organizations utilize the internet and operating systems to deal with core business processes, networking security concerns are on the rise - particularly for those sectors dealing with sensitive financial and personal data. Hence, the call for Ethical Hackers and Penetration Testing is notable. Identifying vulnerabilities is vital for many and ongoing - as the Black Hats diversify systems need to be consistently assessed.

Looking For Hacker Training?

Hacking or penetrating into the information system in order to gather details of the organization is rampant these days, and this calls for help to protect the system. Entering or sneaking into a system to check for any faults in the system is termed as ethical hacking.

This is done by professionals who are employed by companies to check if the system can be penetrated into and also to devise ways of preventing such activities. This is why hacker training is very popular these days, and there are many workshops that are held for certified ethical hacker training. Shopping on the net is the best option if you are looking for hacker training.

ETHICAL HACKER TRAINING

The hacker training that is imparted by professionals during the workshops trains people to think and act differently. Hacking is a term that is synonymous with computers, but that is not the only system that can be hacked. People can hack into telephones, mobiles and other similar networking systems. In order to get ethical hacker training, you can also research tools that are available on the net. Some of the tools that are really good are not available free of cost on the net, but you should have some of them. They are Snoopers, Compilers, Hex file editors, and APIs.

Along with these basic tools, in order to get ethical hacking training, you should also garner techniques that help you in scripting, formatting and editing of the disk and accordingly help you to disassemble. Programming is a basic requirement in ethical hacking training. There is a lot of programming that is involved in the process of hacking and therefore you should be familiar with programming languages. Another requirement is the familiarity of Windows, UNIX, Linux and other operating systems.

Successful certified ethical hacker training

Apart from the above-mentioned requirements, there are some general requirements in order to make the training a successful one. The first and most important requirement is learning in a group. There needs to be a lot of discussion and exchange of ideas when you are getting training for such a certification. The next important thing is for you to get involved in some live projects. Hands-on experience is always better than what you read and understand from the books. It is always important to start a project from scratch and build on it so that you understand every minute detail of the working. The next very important step is to make complete use of the internet. This is the place where you can get all the information you would ever need and you also need to learn every required aspect of the net like making Boolean searches.

Every time you stumble upon a good site you need to bookmark it so that you can visit it later when you need it. These days there are many institutions that provide training for hacking and if you are looking for hacker training then you need to surf the net to find all the required information.

There is an increase in the dependence on computers and the internet these days. Along with this dependence, there is also an increase in crimes that are related to the cyber world. Hacker training helps counter the implications.

HOW TO BECOME A PROFESSIONAL ETHICAL HACKER

Also known as Intrusion Testing or Penetration Testing, Ethical Hacking is a computer and network-based expertise to detect loopholes in an IT system and fix them accordingly. The ethical hackers are well-versed in computer and networking algorithms. Such experts intrude into security systems on behalf of their owners to ensure that the system is not vulnerable to malicious hackers. Ethical hackers are employed to enhance the safety potentiality of a computer system to specifically prevent external threats from attacking it. With internet consumption skyrocketing worldwide, ethical hackers have become an integral workforce of any IT security industry today.

Industry Status

In the United States alone, the ethical hacking was expected to be a US $3.8 billion industry. It was also estimated that around 77,000 ethical hackers will be required every year in India. Sadly, the country produces just 15000 such hackers in a year currently. No doubt, ethical hacking is mounting at a very significant pace worldwide. It, therefore, offers a wide spectrum of lucrative job opportunities for those who want to make a career in it.

Skill Sets Required

First of all, the aspirant should have a good grasp of writing programming languages such as C+, C++, Perl, Python, and Ruby. An experience with Web Applications, PHP, and

Microsoft.NET will be very useful for the aspirants. If you are well-versed in Assembly Language, you can become a part of a team working as Disassembled Binaries Analyst. Knowledge of Operating Systems (Microsoft Windows, Linux, etc.) and Network Devices (switches, routers, firewall, etc.) are also very useful in this respect. A basic familiarity with TCP/IP protocols such as SMTP, ICMP, and HTTP is also vital. The aspirants should have good soft skills including adaptability and resourcefulness to troubleshoot any unforeseeable snags during testing software and systems.

Remuneration

An ethical hacker with no prior working experience in this field can work as an intern for months with an annual package of Rs 2.5 lakhs in India. Thus the rate of growth in remuneration increases as per the work experience increases. A professional with more than 5 years of experience can work in an information security industry on a handsome annual package of Rs 12 lakhs. Ethical hacking can be one of the lucrative career options for the aspirants. With mounting popularity worldwide, the aspirant can work in a reputed IT Company in any part of the world. The scope of ethnic hacking is very large and wide today.

Are denial of service, intrusion detection, and hacking web servers your ideas for fun? If yes, then taking a career as an Information Security Professional or an Ethical Hacker will be the right choice. An ethical hacker is also known as a white hat hacker who works legally to control the vulnerabilities in a computer or a network. One can be in high demand at the organizational level by owning the professional certification -

Certified Ethical Hacker (CEH).

What is Certified Ethical Hacker (CEH)?

A CEH is an ethical hacker who determines network vulnerabilities and takes preventive countermeasures to avoid data loss. A Certified Ethical Hacker (CEH) certificate issued by the International Council of E-Commerce Consultants (EC-Council) certifies the information security skills of a professional. This credential is vendor-neutral and globally accepted.

Who can benefit?

The course is significantly beneficial for individuals working as website administrators, security professionals, auditors, and professionals dealing with network infrastructure.

Ways to earn the certification

The two ways offered by EC-Council to earn this certification are as follows:

Accredited Training Center (ATC): One can attend a five-day online or on-site training program at any of the ATCs. At the completion, the candidate is eligible to attempt the web-based Prometric Prime Exam.

Self-study: One can attempt for the exam by going through the provided self-study material and showing at least two years of information security related work experience, endorsed by the employer. If that is not the case, one can send the educational details along with a request for consideration.

How to apply?

The steps to apply for this certification are as follows:

Complete the application form by getting your employer verification. Attach a copy of any government-approved identification such as a passport. Submit the scanned copy of the form and documents. Remit a non-refundable eligibility application fee of 100.00 USD. The approval from EC-Council generally takes two weeks.

Version 8 is the latest certificate provided as of late 2013. Candidates who go through the ATC mode of examination appear for exam code 312-50. If the candidates go through the self-study route, they are eligible for exam EC0-350 at an Authorized Prometric Testing Centre (APTC).

The exam is comprised of 125 multiple-choice questions. During the four-hour exam, candidates will scan, test, hack, and secure their systems. Candidates must secure 70 percent marks to come out with flying colors. Once the candidate is certified, the welcome kit will reach after eight weeks.

Strengthen your resume with CEH certification! A qualification as a certified ethical hacker can get you far. It not only demonstrates you have a vast amount of knowledge on internet security and networking, it helps you recognize the flaws in the system and how hackers get through. It's by far the best way to protect your network - by understanding how to break through. Thus then you can take the necessary precautions.

The certified ethical hacker (CEH) is provided by the EC council. It teaches the necessary network and security area of ethical hacking, which uses the same techniques as hackers for ethical purposes: to secure a network. After all, to defeat a hacker, you must think like one!

The CEH is one of the most comprehensive vendor-neutral certificates on ethical hacking. With many modules, it covers anything an ethical hacker might need to know, from the scanning, testing to the final hacking process. The CEH is the best way to become an ethical hacker, as it gives you the top ethical hacker accreditation in the industry.

The CEH begins by teaching the learner about the latest security systems, as to hack it you need expert level knowledge on the security system itself. Learners will then begin to understand the way in which perimeter defenses work before they learn to hack. As well as hacking, the certified ethical hacker teaches the network and security expert how to secure a system in a number of events and other security issues, such as viruses and how they are created, and Trojans. It will also provide with a sound knowledge of hacking laws, enabling you to understand the security and ethical hacking process in conjunction with law.

With security, the best way to protect your system is to know how your enemy works. Putting their efforts and knowledge into practice can help you stay one step ahead of them, avoiding unwanted penetration of your systems. Training in the CEH can be done in a number of ways, from attending intensive courses that last around 5 days to training at home using computer-based training over a period of a year. Whatever you choose, the CEH is taught by top experts in the field and enables you to gain experience and understanding of the ethical hacking process.

As time has passed, we have been able to drastically evolve and improve the level of technology. But with the evolution of technology, it has also left behind its residue and that has turned out to be the vulnerability and the loopholes of the technology which could lead to a situation of hacking, where the important information and data might be accessed in the purpose of theft, modification, or destruction, etc. So, these hackers turned out to be the troubled geniuses of the information systems where they can combat and breach the enabled security in your device and can leave you mugged.

In recent times, the need for information security also increased, where someone can help in preventing situations like these and can save you from moments of apocalypse. Now, these people who are the nemesis to their unethical counterparts have been able to help us in providing proactive information security and save us from going into sleepless nights. They ensure the safety and security of our data and information and guard it from any catastrophe. We call them "Ethical Hackers". So, how does it sound to be an ethical hacker? Does it fancy you? If yes, there are a few brief points you might want to look at and understand to be a professional ethical hacker.

You need to understand the various kinds of hacking, which can be classified into White Hat, Grey Hat, and non-ethical hacking. You need to evaluate all three to understand them very well. Only deep knowledge can help in combating any sort of breach or unauthorized access in the information system. Also, it can help you in ensuring the proactive security to the systems while discovering the vulnerability of the information systems. A deep knowledge and potent skills can help you in becoming a good ethical hacker.

You need to identify the basic requirements to be an ethical hacker. Whether you need to undertake a course or a diploma or you need any other licensing done. Make sure you do your homework well and then go hit the bullseye.

Upon successful evaluation of the basic requirements, you need to run the horses of your brain where you need to decide whether would you like to work in hardware or software securities? Believe me, this field is so vast, and you don't want to take the chances of riding on two boats at a time. Master a formula first and then go for another. So, choose it carefully.

Along with your conventional diploma or the certificate program, don't forget the UNIX operating system. It is known as the bible of hacking, and it is known as the original operating system developed and designed by the hackers only. Make sure you learn it well.

Once you acquired your knowledge, it's time to know your strength and your weaknesses. Now, give yourself a try and implement your knowledge by practically doing things on your own system. Write down the complete analysis and then go for another round. Go until you succeed and turn highly skilled.

There are many things that are possible at a click these days, thanks to the services of the internet. But along with this, there are also a number of risks and crimes related to the internet that have now increased, and one of the most serious ones is hacking.

Hacking refers to entering computer systems of companies in order to get information. This is illegal and dangerous to the company and all the information that is kept with the company records. In order to prevent such an intrusion, companies are now appointing professionals who are experts in preventing hacking, and these professionals are called white hat hackers or ethical hackers. This is why hacker training is becoming so popular.

Significance of Programming in Developing Certified Ethical Hacker Training Skills

The main functionality expected of a person undergoing ethical hacker training is to check the information system of an organization to test if there are any flaws in the system and also to check if there are any viruses. The certified professional is also expected to find solutions and make necessary changes so that penetration into the system is not possible by any unauthorized person. In order to be a successful ethical hacker, the person taking the ethical hacker training needs to have some skills.

One of the most important skills is the knowledge of programming skills. A person who aims at getting certified ethical hacker training needs to have knowledge of programming languages like Java, C++, Perl, Python, and Lisp. If you are just starting afresh, then it is a good option to learn Python first because it is easy to learn and less complicated compared to the other programs. After you learn this program, you can go on to learn Lisp, Perl, Java, and C.

Other Required Skills

Apart from the above-mentioned skills, there are some other skills that need to be picked up as a part of honing imparted certified ethical hacker training skills. One of them is learning and understanding UNIX. This is very important because it is the very basis of the internet and without learning this operating system, rewrites and modifications are not possible. The best way of learning it is by practicing on the Linux or UNIX that is on your own computer. The next skill is to learn HTML which is very important in ethical hacker training.

If you need to have hacker training, the knowledge of how to write HTML programs is a necessity. In order to understand all this and to make the ethical hacking training effective, it is necessary to be fluent in English too. This is because all the resources that are available in this regard are accessible in English and if you are not fluent in the language then no amount of training can make you an expert. Also, you need to develop a habit of reading and gathering information from the net because the more informed you are, the better. There are many institutes that train people but a lot of work and research needs to be done on your own.

ETHICAL HACKER TRAINING WORKSHOPS

Ethical hacker training workshops are being held to update IT professionals in countering fraudulent hacking attempts. The professionals are kept abreast with the latest developments in security systems against cybercrimes.

Many key concepts related to ethical hacking are covered in these workshops, including addressing Trojans, security related to wireless systems and the web, and cracking of software. The course is structured in a comprehensive manner that includes all the required information for hacker training. The modules offer hands-on experience to face the dangers that may surface in the real world.

The workshops equip the candidates undergoing the ethical hacker training in a manner that they become aware of how to check systems and also correct mistakes if any. They also train the candidates to protect a system from any future intrusions and attacks. Though hacking by itself is illegal, ethical hacking helps to keep illegal and fraudulent elements away from your system. These workshops on ethical hacking training help in this regard. Therefore, when you undergo certified ethical hacker training, you are trained to handle all the untoward situations in this regard that may raise their ugly heads at any point in time.

There are some key qualities that are required by a person who is interested in hacker training. The most important quality is to be curious. The more curious you are, the more you are going to be interested in looking past the obvious. This is bound to help you understand and know the details of the accounts and the files that are a part of the entire information system.

The next quality required is to be a voracious reader. You need to be well-read with regards to all the information that is available on these topics. The more reading you do, the more informed you are going to be.

You also have to develop and nurture the urge to experiment. You should have no fear whatsoever to try out something that is new and out of the way. It is sometimes through such kind of behavior that you stumble upon things that are unknown to others. Try and change things in the system and see what happens when doing so.

The other very important thing when undergoing certified ethical hacker training is for the candidate to be constantly open to generating backups. When you try out new things, there are chances that errors will unfold and they could ruin many subsequent events.

In order to avoid something untoward during training, you need to take all precautions and ensure at the very onset that all your data is stored elsewhere. These are some of the requirements of training for an ethical hacker. The training is delivered by professionals who help to inculcate the qualities even if they are not ingrained.

With the number of cybercrimes on the rise these days, the need for professionals who are part of ethical hacker training is also increasing. Due to this increase, the techniques deployed for ethical hacking are also constantly being upgraded by the experts in the field.

When a system is hacked into by someone who only does so to tamper, the loss caused to the company as a whole is immeasurable! Very important and classified information can be lost and leaked to other competitors, and this could result in major fiscal and business-centric and sensitive losses for the company. These are some of the reasons why hacker training and especially ethical hacking training is gaining so much importance these days. There are many modules within certified ethical hacker training that make the hacker capable of protecting a system from all forms of threats.

What is the importance of ethical hacker training?

Due to the increase in the need for such professionals, ethical hacker training is gaining a lot of ground these days. Once they are trained, candidates are able to penetrate into systems of companies to recognize the problems and find solutions to any bridges and gaps identified in the system. Ethical hackers are also known as white hat hackers and what they specialize in are ways in which bad-hacking or fraudulent hacking can be avoided. They are geared to address techniques required for anti-hacking programs.

These white hat hackers help to keep unethical hackers at bay. They are trained within modules to identify people who hack systems for the sake of destroying them and causing trouble to an organization. With the right techniques, these candidates are then trained to keep such frauds away from the system and protect the system from any further attack. Professionals from ethical hacking training workshops protect the information system of a company from hackers who steal passwords, send extortion threats through emails and adopt very criminal methods of extracting funds and assets. People who go through the certified ethical hacker training also get equipped to protect a system from threats that are launched to destroy the system through infected programs and people who steal internet time from your account.

What is the content of the modules within certified ethical hacker training?

Apart from the above-mentioned threats, the professional who goes through the certified ethical hacker training is equipped to protect a company from major threats like defacement on the web, complete takeover of the company, launching of websites on behalf of the company but containing information that is completely distasteful and wrong and even using content to run down the organization. Candidates are taught through training modules delivered by professionals who are adept at IT techniques to counter hacking attempts. Tricksters are known to send and receive mails that are criminal in nature and this could be done in the name of the company.

There are also cases of harassment through the net and forging of websites. The ethical hacker, once trained, protects the company from dangers of robbery and mismanagement of information and also cash and credit card numbers and manipulation of accounts. In some cases, they also tackle identification of the base point of spam mails sent and theft of records that are stored in the electronic form and also theft of hardware and software of the computer. There are also some serious problems like morphing and bombing through emails and stalking addressed at these workshops. All this boils down to just one fact that it is your responsibility to check if your system is safe and protected and this can only be done with the help of people who have done hacker training and thus are trained to handle such situations.

Hacking has become a growing problem these days, with more and more systems being hacked on a regular basis. This needs to be avoided and the information system of the company needs to be protected from such intrusion. This is where ethical hacker training comes in.

This is one of the most frequently asked questions about the world of ethical hacking. Do you need to learn how to program to become a penetration tester? My answer would be "You are NOT going to be a good hacker."

Ethical Hacking is a loophole for us to do what we love and actually get paid to do it. Every hacker I have ever talked to got their start with an intense curiosity about computers, networks, etc. and how they all work together. Programming languages allow us to create anything we can imagine. If I was an architect, I could design any shape building I wanted, BUT it had to adhere to the laws of physics so that it was structurally sound. In programming, there are NO laws. ANYTHING can be created.

When I got my start in computers, I took every programming class I could and read every single book I could. I became obsessed with all that could be done on a computer. Programming skills are what set apart real computer gurus and the script kiddies who just run programs (they didn't write themselves) to wreak havoc.

There are plenty of topics within Ethical Hacking that require no programming skills whatsoever. But if you truly are looking into a career as an Ethical Hacker, you are like me and want to learn as much as you can about everything computing. There are hundreds of programming languages to choose from, compiled languages like C to scripting languages like Python and Ruby that are interpreted on the spot. Occasionally, I will even dive deeper and play around with esoteric languages such as Befunge, where the whole point of the language is to be completely obfuscated. It turns programming even the simplest of programs into a mind-challenging puzzle.

Whatever your interest is, programming languages are necessary for a fuller understanding of how computers work, process things, and communicate with each other. The next important question is: which programming languages should I learn to stay competitive?

The answer to this will vary from programmer to programmer. My advice is to learn a language or two from each category. You'll begin to find that most programming languages work similarly but with varied syntax.

Starting off, I would recommend the way I started my programming career, with Java. It is an extremely powerful Object-Oriented programming language and is widely used in today's world. If you're beginning to feel comfortable with Java, I would suggest stepping it up and trying to tackle C++ or get down even closer to machine code with C.

SECURITY - AN ETHICAL HACKER

If an online company is large enough, they might employ a white hat hacker. Typically, when you hear the word "hacker", it conjures up someone who, with ill intent, will search for ways to mine your company data and destroy or replace data. A white hat hacker is someone who could use their abilities to harm your business, but they make the choice to help uncover security failings in your system. The reason this is helpful to many companies is that if they can revamp their online store to close backdoor entrance to would-be hackers, then their company data can be safeguarded and customers can experience an even greater level of trust in the company. Maybe this explains why so many of the larger online businesses seem to have less downtime and experience fewer problems. Most hackers know they will have a harder time getting into these systems than smaller companies that may not have the resources to investigate every possible security leak.

That being said, it is important for online businesses to make sure they take proper precautions by installing antivirus protection, spyware removal tools, and firewall protection. Hackers don't always target a specific site so much as they create software that looks to find an entrance and then they investigate what can be found inside those sites they can infiltrate. Some hackers have said they mean no harm; they simply are curious and have found new ways of finding out information. Too often this is information they should not have access to.

The truth is some hackers consider what they do as a means

of making the online environment safer for individuals and businesses. If they can disable an online store or take over a website, they figure this proves what they have been saying all along - sites are not as safe online as some think. To their credit, what hackers have learned has often resulted in a better way to secure websites in general, but the other, and even more important, side to this security coin is that online business must remain vigilant in the safeguard of their company data.

This whole process is a bit like the progression from small town America where everyone left their doors unlocked because it just wasn't polite to take something that didn't belong to you to the point where alarms are tripped if someone tries to enter your home after you set the alarm. Things have changed in an online sales environment and applying strong security measures to your site is not only in your best interest but also the interest of your customers who place their trust in your ability to safeguard their data.

ARE WE STILL BEHIND THE HACKERS?

The recent developments regarding the Large Hadron Collider - a machine built to try and figure out how the Big Bang happened - were overshadowed not long after the experiment started by news that hackers had managed to access one of the computers being used for the experiment to register their distaste at what was going on. While the experiment itself was unharmed, the general public cannot now find out what is going on because the website related to it has been hacked and cannot be accessed.

So in answer to the question posed by the title of this piece, the answer would appear to be that we are still some way behind them. Hackers act on all kinds of motives, and one of the reasons why they have so many opportunities to hack into websites is that some people think they are only at risk if their site takes payment information from others. That simply isn't the case, because some hackers do what they do simply to compromise internet security, or to make a point of how easy it can be to hack into a facility. There are numerous examples of hackers managing to get past the defenses of government websites and those relating to parts of the law, so there is clearly no single reason why websites are continuing to be hacked into and exposed as being insecure as a result.

But there are services out there that use ethical hacking to expose and plug weaknesses in websites, and it is these services that should be used more and more if we are to keep on top of the hackers, rather than it being the other way around. After all, wouldn't you rather pay the money to get an ethical hacker to try and break through your defenses so they can remedy any problems you may have, than wait for someone who isn't so ethical to do it for you? In the latter case, you won't get any help to make sure no one else gets through - all you will get is hassle and the problems they leave behind.

Just as people are coming up with new ways to break through systems, so the ethical hacking companies are developing ways to combat them, and if you want your business to be as secure as it can possibly be then you owe it to yourself, your staff, and your clients to pay for the best knowledge out there today. So in reality, it is perfectly true that a lot of companies are still behind the hackers and are running the risk of being hacked into and subjected to a lot of damage every single day. It is those businesses who have essentially invested the money in their future that will remain as secure as it is possible to be, as they have hired the best computer security company they can afford to make sure they are fully protected both now and in the future.

And why try and keep up with all the developments yourself when you can hire the professionals to do it for you?

Perhaps the question should really be, how long could they bring down your business for?

It's an alarming thought, but in truth a single hacker with the right knowledge could seriously damage your business to the point that you wouldn't be able to function in any real way for several days, perhaps even longer.

It's clear that you have a responsibility to make sure your

business is as safe as it possibly can be. In this sense, the best stance to take is to assume that yes, a hacker could indeed bring down your whole business. Are you prepared to let that happen?

Of course not - and this is why you need to put in place adequate measures to protect yourself from attack by hackers with all kinds of motives for doing what they do.

If you still aren't convinced, it may pay you to do a little research on the consequences that hacking can bring. A famous example occurred some ten years ago to Pixar Animation. An email purporting to come from the CEO (but actually coming from the hacker who had managed to get into the system) was sent to every employee detailing exactly how much each of them got paid.

Now if this happened to your business, how would you deal with the fallout? It's true that this kind of event does not have a direct effect on your clients, and if the hacker is just trying to prove a point and isn't interested in having the personal information of your employees then their personal information is 'safe' (if you can really call it that.)

But how do you think your employees would feel if they knew that confidential details about their employment had been made available to everyone else working for you? It's clear that you would have some serious damage limitation to do, and the issue of trust that is gradually built up between a business and its employees would be blown out of the water by one single email.

Many people believe that all they need to do is ensure that

their customers' details are safe and their payment details (if the company processes transactions online) are not compromised, but the above example shows that just isn't the case. Hackers are capable of bringing down your business in more ways than you might think; which is why getting outside help is very often a good idea.

So who should you turn to? In short, you need to focus on engaging the services of a trusted business with an excellent track record in providing internet security. This type of business has the wealth of knowledge and skills that you need to protect you against hackers of all types and descriptions, right around the clock.

There are plenty of companies around who have been built up by so-called 'ethical hackers', who make a point of using their considerable skills to help other businesses rather than bring them down. They know exactly how to breach a system, and will try to break into yours for the purposes of plugging all the vulnerable spots they find.

The increase in computer and mobile technology has led to greater threats in security. This could be in the form of viruses that can crash the system and allow easy access to confidential data. With the rapid modernisation in technology across corporations, how does one stop security intrusions from taking place? The job of securing systems and mobile devices can be best left to a trained ethical hacker. Such a person would have trained himself on an ethical hacking course.

The job of an ethical hacker is to systematically penetrate the computer network of an organization in order to determine the security vulnerabilities of the same. Whatever turns out to be the vulnerability of the system is determined and then accordingly fixed by the IT department of the organization. If these vulnerabilities are not fixed, they could be potentially exploited by a malicious hacker.

The methods used by an ethical and a malicious hacker are nearly the same. Both have almost the same knowledge in terms of programming. However, the intentions are what really differentiate one from the other. A traditional hacker uses illegal techniques to bypass a system's defences, whereas the ethical hacker makes use of legal techniques. The ethical hacker is given permission by the organization to invade security systems. In addition, this person also documents threats and vulnerabilities, providing an action plan on how to fix overall security.

Where are vulnerabilities usually found?

Usually, when a large number of software are being used on computers, it gives chances of infection from viruses. These viruses are actually illegal programs which can supply information to other sources. Poor or improper system configurations are liable to have infections and vulnerabilities. Any kind of hardware or software flaws, as well as operational weaknesses in technical processes, can lead to program corruption.

International standards followed by ethical hackers

There are various standards in the industry which allow companies to carry out penetration testing. One of these is

Payment Card Industry Data Security Standard. This consists of a globally recognized set of policies and procedures meant to optimize securities of credit, debit as well as cash card transactions. It also protects cardholders from misuse of personal information.

Large companies like IBM have large teams of employees as ethical hackers. Many global firms also offer ethical hacking in the form of a course. Another organization called as Trustwave Holdings Inc. has its own Ethical Hacking lab which can explore potential vulnerabilities in ATMs, POS devices and different kinds of surveillance systems.

An ethical hacking course provides all the various advanced tools and techniques used by security professionals to breach the vulnerabilities of systems in an organization. The course makes you think like a hacker and explore a situation from a hacker's mindset. More can be learned from a cybersecurity training course.

HOW HACKERS USE SOCIAL ENGINEERING TO GET INSIDE

Whether you call them hackers, crackers, or cyber criminals, it doesn't matter. What does matter is that whatever you call them, they're looking for a way into your network! You may not realize it, but hackers are scanning your internet connection looking for an opening. What will they do if they find one? They'll launch an attack against that opening to see if they can exploit a vulnerability that will allow them to remotely execute some commands, thereby giving them access to your network. But it all starts with scanning your network.

Automated Tools Are a Wonderful Thing

Cyber criminals don't scan each individual network on the internet one by one. They have automated tools that randomly scan every IP address on the internet. Hackers aren't lazy people - just very efficient. And very intelligent. The tools they use can be preloaded with a range of internet addresses to scan. As this tool finds an internet address with certain openings, it produces a list of the address and the opening. This list is then fed into another tool that actively tries to exploit that opening with various programs. If no exploit works, the hacker's program moves on to the next potential victim.

When you see the scanning activity in your firewall logs, you'll know where you're being scanned from and what they're trying to target. Armed with that data, you should check to see if you're running software that uses that port and if it has any newly discovered openings. If you are using software listening on that scanned port and there is a patch available, you should have that patch applied immediately - because the hackers may know something you don't.

NOTE: It's been our experience that many businesses patch their Microsoft Windows software but rarely do they check for patches for all the other software used in the business.

As stated, you'll see this activity in your firewall logs - that is, if someone is actually reviewing your firewall logs.

"Oh, my firewall has logs?"

However, when most business owners are asked about their firewall logs, the typical response is usually something like, "Oh, my firewall has logs?" Yes, all firewalls produce log files. Most of them only show what's been blocked, which is like showing pictures of all the thieves that are in prison, while the bank down the street is being robbed.

Wouldn't you want to see all traffic? This produces more work, but if your firewall only logs activity it knows about, your security is totally dependent on the ability of your firewall and the way it's configured.

Many firewall companies want to reduce their number of tech support calls. Their business model revolves around having tech support available, but in the process, they're also seeking ways of reducing the number of times people call in. This isn't necessarily a bad thing, but when their products have fewer features, thus fewer benefits as a result - that is a bad thing.

Most firewalls designed for the small business market lack features that most small businesses would benefit from. Many of them have all the technical buzzwords like "deep packet inspection", "spyware prevention", "intrusion detection" and many others, however, they don't go into the level of detail needed to be effective.

First, many firewalls that are "designed" for small businesses start with companies that have 100-250 users. These might be considered small businesses by the Bureau of Labor Statistics, but for technology purposes, companies of this size have their own IT staff (96% do). Not just one IT person, but an IT staff, which means that someone is probably responsible for security. If not, they'll have someone train them in the proper setup, installation, and monitoring of security appliances.

The businesses we consider small have anywhere from 3-50 PCs. The companies at the higher end of this scale might have someone dedicated to handling IT issues. But this person is usually so inundated with PC support issues that they have little time "left over" to effectively monitor firewall logs.

Towards the lower end of this scale, they usually have either an outside person or firm responsible or they have an employee who "is pretty good with computers" who has other responsibilities as well. Rarely will these small businesses have someone watching the firewall logs on a consistent basis. Someone might look them over if there's an issue, but these logs rotate when filled so the valuable information might be lost before it's ever reviewed. And that's a shame. Without reviewing the logs, you have no idea what or who is trying to get in with which or what.

The Inside Scoop

Though the word hacker conventionally brings to mind images of shady criminals working in dingy rooms, ex-crackers are gaining prominence in the field of professional hacking as well! Take the case of Joe Magee, a twenty-three-year-old ex-cracker who was recently hired as the Chief Security Officer of Top Layer Networks, a security products company!

This company is among many who are realizing that hackers have immense skills that, when used positively, can improve the way we look at computing and make it more efficient.

Magee's life story is heavily intertwined with computing; his parents bought him a Mac after watching him analyze the family VCR. Soon enough, Magee became a computer whiz, curious to learn everything about computing. Magee started his first computer-oriented job at fourteen with Philadelphia's Globe Times and from then on continued to provide his immense technical acumen to numerous firms.

Magee's story is an inspiring one that describes exactly what you need to become a successful professional hacker: dedication and an immense interest in all aspects of computing. Evidently, hackers are of great use in a world where technology is quickly becoming an intricate part in all aspects of life; it is thus a promising career choice for those interested.

Sweet Sensations

A career as a professional hacker definitely has its perks: imagine being able to walk into any room and floor people with your multifaceted computer knowledge! Plus, hacking still holds conventional notions of mystery and drama and you'll easily be the most popular person in the room, surrounded by people dying to know what you really do! A hacker also comes with serious bragging rights as you can publicize your ability to break past strong security barriers and easily be the life and soul of any gathering.

Hacking is a great career choice if you're intensely interested in the computer world as it allows you to delve deep into the intricate elements of computing. It's a job that allows you to work from anywhere including the comforts of your home, in your favorite chair, which is a good choice if you're the type who does not like the daily commute to and from the office.

You can also relish the fact that you are doing the world a great service: computers are used in nearly every field of life and they are easy targets for malicious crackers. By becoming a professional hacker, you prevent the proliferation of these spiteful people and thus ensure a smooth functioning system which entails numerous crucial processes around the world. This is definitely something to be proud of!

Professional hacking is not a regular IT-oriented job; hackers are hired by several government agencies and often get to hack into top-secret systems that no one else has access to; this side of the job is not only rewarding but extremely fascinating as you will get to be involved in the foundations of numerous actions that take place in the world and delight in the knowledge that you helped things proceed in a safe manner.

Hurdles and Challenges

This career incorporates a great deal of manual work and time spent in front of a computer. You'll have to spend months trying to work through complex security codes, and this involves a great deal of mathematical and technical know-how.

Like many IT-oriented jobs, professional hacking is extremely demanding, and given time constraints, may be a severe strain on employees. There will be days when you will be unable to open your eyes due to weariness, but you'll still be expected to solve a complicated computer problem within the given time.

This career demands a great deal of patience, as the workload is complicated, and in many cases, you will have to spend much time trying to get through it. Moreover, the job comes with numerous negative stereotypes, which can be irritating if you're an ethical hacker just trying to do your job; it can be an obstacle within itself. Hacking has not been completely accepted yet, and some still view hackers as criminal and will treat you as such.

Fruits of Labor
Primary

You can expect your salary to be anywhere between $53,000 and $70,000 in the early years. Currently, professional hackers are paid an average of $60,000, but this depends heavily on experience and the firm. Generally, the longer you work in the industry, the more competent you become to handle complicated computer security issues, and hence, the more you earn. This may not be exorbitant for the amount of work you'll be expected to put in, but it certainly will cover many of your pressing needs!

Perhaps the key advantage of this career is the style of work: it is less formal, and you can work based heavily on your personal requirements. You can also work from home, and this is a great benefit!

Secondary

Obviously, being a hacker is a great career choice if you're brimming with technical know-how and don't know what to do with it. You'll get a great sense of superiority when you finally break through an exceedingly strong security barrier, and this is definitely an unmatched high! You'll also broaden your knowledge with more hands-on experience, which will help you create systems for yourself that are highly efficient and suit your needs.

The best advantage, however, is that you will never be a victim of cracking if you're a good hacker! By hacking your own system, you'll be able to spot weaknesses early on, and you can be smug about the fact that you've outsmarted those malicious thieves!

Essential Tools:

From Home

Practice obviously makes perfect, and all good hackers start from what they have at home! Try hacking your own system to learn how it works, and this will give you a general idea of the hacking process. There are numerous websites and blogs that give you first-hand experience of what it is like to be a hacker and what you can do to get started, and these should be used extensively to get a feel of the career.

Learn computer languages and codes thoroughly by taking apart the software you have, including games and operating systems. Experience is the determining factor for wages and makes you more aware of the hacking process; it's thus a crucial element of your training.

From School

You could take the Certified Ethical Hacker course and receive a certification in how to find weaknesses in systems and solve them. This course is gaining popularity and presents a systematic means of learning the ropes.

A degree in computer science will obviously be helpful for a focused appreciation of the subject, but most hackers learn from home due to their intense curiosity. A degree will only give you a fixed amount of information; that 'something extra' which differentiates between a highly-paid hacker and a low-paid hacker often has a lot to do with hands-on experience. Therefore, you should definitely be working on hacking at home while also doing a certified course. Certification adds credibility, and this is what some firms look for. This is why you shouldn't negate a computer science degree; it should certainly be undertaken alongside first-hand experience.

At the Job

As with many occupations in the IT industry, perseverance and dedication are cardinal principles. Hacking is no easy job, and it will certainly take you a while before you solve the problems set before you. However, if you maintain your composure and work steadily throughout, you should be able to prosper in the industry and make enough to buy yourself something special!

Talk to professional hackers if you find them; they're usually labeled as security analysts and are often helpful in giving valuable advice. Hacking is like any other career, it will demand a lot out of you. And though the financial rewards may not be as high as some of the other IT careers, it is definitely a field that holds great importance and interest. Hacking is a great alternative to cracking as you get paid for your services, and you can still claim to be smarter than the creators of the program you test! It is thus a good career choice for those with an avid interest in computing.

Ensuring that you have adequate network protection is vital, but protecting your system from hackers who use social engineering to get inside should also be a priority. Even the best employee may create system vulnerabilities if they aren't aware of the threat, and companies often overlook this hacking angle.

Hackers can be smooth operators. They may call looking for advice, offering flattery in the attempt to gain your employees' trust. They use this connection to talk their way into getting information about the security your company has in place and the programs you run. They may also prey on your employees' confidence in the network in order to gain specific details and shortcomings about your system operations. By using social engineering to obtain even small amounts of information about how your system operates and what programs you use, the hackers can run software on their end that will not only give them greater detail on your system, but it can show them how to get inside.

Suavely manipulating an individual isn't the only social engineering method hackers use. Some hackers are far more direct. It's hard to believe, but they may directly call a business and impersonate an authority in the company. Employees can be easily swayed by a person issuing a direct request in an authoritative tone. Employees have been known to do what the hacker says because they believe they are being asked on behalf of the company. They may change passwords or issue new ones, allowing the hacker access to your system. The hacker may start small and simply ask for access to "their" email account, which is generally that of a system administrator. Once they have access to this account, they can issue credible commands to gain further access to and control over your business' systems.

No one wants to think that getting access to their company's system could be so easy, but it can and does happen. Using these tricks to gain access to business networks is actually quite common. The key to limiting this risk is comprehensive training for your employees so they learn to see through the hackers' ploys.

How can you help limit the risk of these threats compromising your security?

- Educate your employees about how hackers utilize social engineering in order to obtain access to a system. Your employees cannot fight this problem if they don't know it exists.

- Decide what information about your system is too risky to make public, and train your employees not to release this data.

- Formalize procedures for obtaining and changing passwords and access to email accounts. If you can ensure that no outside party is gaining passwords, you've thwarted one major hacker tool.

Your company cannot fight this problem if it isn't aware of it, but once your employees understand the risks they'll be in a better position to fight it. Training your employees is a small step that will net large results in limiting your business' vulnerability.

CONCLUSION

When most people think about computer security, the word hacker comes to mind. Another word that is also associated with bad computer behavior is cracker, and most of the time, the two words are used interchangeably, but they are not the same thing.

A hacker is a person who has a great deal of computing skills and enjoys the challenges of solving technical issues. This includes breaking and infiltrating computers and networks. The aim of hackers is not to cause damage, but the technical aspects and how to overcome them fascinate them, and they see it as learning and as a status symbol amongst the hacker community.

An individual does not give himself the title hacker, but it is left up to the community to bestow that title if the person has demonstrated the required knowledge and proved it. A hacker feels that information should be free, so they document how they went about overcoming certain difficulties so others can learn from them. This sharing raises the status of the individual concerned, and as a whole, the community benefits.

Unlike a hacker, the aim of a cracker is to cause mischief and gain some benefit by causing harm to the owner of the computer or network broken into, e.g., by stealing credit card details or installing some malicious software.

Hackers see crackers as lowlifes and try very hard to distinguish themselves from them, but this is not easy, especially when the media insists on calling everybody a hacker. The difference between a hacker and a cracker might not seem a lot to the average person because after all, both of them break into unauthorized computers and networks, but in reality, there is a big difference because what matters is what the person does after he/she infiltrates a network.

You're probably familiar with the phrase, "An ounce of prevention is worth a pound of cure." If you've ever been victimized by pesky, covert computer predators called hackers, no doubt you can attest to that.

You might wonder why a hacker might want to break into your computer system without your permission. Well, there are a number of reasons, which might include getting access to stored data, the mere challenge of breaking and entering, or simply because they know they can. Once inside, they can wreak havoc by defacing your website, stealing credit card or other confidential information.

Having your computer system compromised can have a devastating impact on your company's reputation, as we saw with the major hack recently experienced by Target, the discount store, where 40 million credit and debit card accounts were stolen.

Regardless of whether you store classified information on your website or not, once hacked, restoring your computer system to its original state can be an arduous task that you'll want to try avoiding at all costs. Here are 7 steps to safeguard your website from being hacked:

Monitor your website. Check your website daily as hackers have a tendency to deface your site or redirect the URL to a pornographic or other questionable site. Google Webmaster Tools (GWMT) can also detect if your website has been compromised by sending you a message with detailed information such as samples of harmful URLs.

Change passwords often. Website owners often make it very easy for hackers to break into their sites because their password and usernames are weak and easily accessible. It is critical that you assign strong passwords to your server login, website login, and email accounts. Be sure to instill good password practices to all users of their accounts.

Back up your website regularly. Make it a practice to back up your website once a week or more often when updates are made. There are some free and fee-based plugins available such as Ready! Backup, Draft Plus, and Backup Buddy for WordPress site.

Keep software updated. It might seem obvious, but it bears repeating... if you access a content management system (CMS) from your computer, an antivirus protection software is a must or you put your system at risk. Hackers are quick to attempt to abuse cracks found in computer security software.

Limit login attempts. Hackers use millions of login combinations to break into your website. By installing login safeguard measures, you can stop hackers in their tracks... or at least make it very difficult for them to force their way into your website. WordPress users can install the plugin, Limit Login Attempts, which keeps banning an IP address after a certain number of failed login attempts.

Use a security certificate. It is a good idea to use an SSL protocol to provide security over the internet when you are passing information between the web server and website. If the communication channel isn't secure, hackers could detect and capture this data to gain access to user accounts and personal data.

Select a reliable web host. Your web host is a crucial resource in your efforts to get your website back up and running as quickly as possible. In addition to their ability to provide emergency help, check to determine if they store recent backup copies of your website files.

Ethical hacker training almost sounds like an oxymoron. How can one be both ethical and a hacker? You will need to gain an understanding of what an ethical hacker is, how they are trained, and what they do to fully comprehend the genius of such a position.

The position is a unique one. The training teaches the same techniques that any hacker would learn to try to infiltrate a computer system. The difference is that they do it to find weaknesses before they can truly be exploited. By finding the weaknesses before they are made accessible to the general public, actual penetration of the system can be avoided. Discovering these weaknesses is merely a way of testing the security of a system.

While the hacking skills may be the same, it is the intent that makes all the difference. While these individuals may still be trying to find a way into the system that would allow them to gain access and control of the inner workings of that system, they do so so that they can then find a way to protect that weakness. They identify the permeable points so that they can be fortified. To stop a hacker, you need to think like one.

The training that such an individual receives must be extensive. A thorough knowledge of how hackers make their way into systems is required so that the defences put in place will be more than adequate to stop any real hacker. If one misses any vulnerability present in the system, then you can be sure that there will be an unethical type out there who will exploit this weakness.

There are a variety of courses offered to assist with this training. While there is no substitute for experience, a comprehensive course in network security can help to prepare an interested person to work in the field. This understanding of both attacks and countermeasures is essential to the position. It includes knowledge of what to do if a system is breached, the investigation of any attempted attacks, and the follow-up on any computer crimes.

Ethical hackers are hired by a company to test the permeability of their network. Their efforts help to keep information and systems safe in a world where high tech crime is becoming more and more common. Finding the holes in a network is not a simple matter because technology of both attack and defence on this level is always changing and advancing.

What was safe and secure six months ago may be easily overcome now. A working knowledge of the latest hacking techniques is a fluid thing. It is always changing. These qualified individuals perform risk analysis and help the various domains to work congruently to assure a high level of security for the whole system. Those who go through training even work to develop the new software that will be put into place once vulnerabilities have been identified and countermeasures have been put in place.

The field of Ethical Hacker training will only grow as more of the business world finds its home on computer systems that are accessible to the public, either by accident or by deliberate intent. The safety of company information, bank information, and personal data all rely on the ability to defend this information from outside attack. This training grooms an individual to think like an outside infiltrator so that they can stay one step ahead and so can the information that he or she was hired to protect. Who knew there was a good kind of hacker?

DON'T GO JUST YET; THERE'S ONE LAST THING TO DO.

If you enjoyed this book or found it useful, I'd be very grateful if you could post a short review of it. Your support truly makes a difference, and I read all the reviews personally so that I can receive your feedback and make this book even better.

Thank you once again for your support!